THE OFFICIAL

RANGERS
FOOTBALL ANNUAL 2001

A Grange Publication

Written and compiled by Jeremy Paxton

£5.99

*Rangers fans turn the Scottish Cup Final orange
in tribute to Dutch manager Dick Advocaat*

A Grange Publication © 2000.

Published by Grange Communications Ltd., Edinburgh.,
under licence from Rangers Football Club.

Design by Brown Wells and Jacobs Ltd. London

Reprographics by TWA Limited. Printed in the EU.

ISBN 1-902704-04-5

HOW TO USE YOUR FLIXPIX!

On every right hand page of this annual there are frames taken from a piece of live action. To make them come to life, simply use your thumb to bend back the pages from this page to the back and then steadily pull back your thumb to let the pages flick over.

INSIDE THIS ANNUAL...

LOOKING AHEAD TO 2000/2001

Rangers manager, Dick Advocaat, is well aware that having secured the Premier League Championship and Scottish Cup last season, the next target for his current Rangers side is success in Europe

Once again, **Rangers** fell agonisingly short of qualification from last season's Champion's League group stage but the performances, particularly the two wins over PSV Eindhoven, the eventual Dutch Champions, were very encouraging. Obviously, you have to beat the best teams in Europe to be successful in the Champion's League, but Advocaat could be forgiven for thinking that he was very unlucky in coming up against such quality sides so early in the competition. For example, **Rangers**' 2-1 aggregate win over Parma in the third qualifying round is even more impressive when you consider that Parma themselves finished fifth in Italy's Serie A. Also, the other two teams in **Rangers**' group, as well as PSV, were Bayern Munich and the eventual finalists, Valencia. Even when **Rangers** dropped out of the Champion's League and into the UEFA Cup, they were paired with Borussia Dortmund, Champions of Europe themselves only two seasons previously, and only went out after a nerve-wracking penalty shoot-out!

With a bit more luck on their side, **Rangers** may well have progressed in either competition. As Advocaat said: "I think we had an excellent campaign. We competed well. With luck and quality, we could perhaps have gone further. We saw Manchester United were beaten by Real Madrid because they had the luck when Roy Keane scored an own goal which changed the game. We were quite close to progressing to the next round of the Champion's League. We must try to stay there for the next couple of years."

However, Advocaat believes that his squad of players is the strongest the Ibrox team has had for some years and with the addition of the new players

in the summer, the side is beginning to show the depth necessary to compete with teams like Barcelona, Lazio and Manchester United. There is also a real sense of camaraderie in the Ibrox changing room, with world-class players like Lorenzo Amoruso, Jorg Albertz, Giovanni van Bronckhorst and Michael Mols prepared to give their all for the blue shirt. These players set the example that the other squad members follow and towards the end of the 1999/2000 season it was obvious that the spirit of the team was superb, especially in the three Old Firm victories over Celtic.

"The team is improving, we have more experience and most of the squad will stay," said Advocaat. "If we play against teams who like to play football, like PSV, Bayern and Parma, then we can compete on the same level. That was the biggest thing last season."

It may well be that **Rangers** will have to follow the route of Manchester United in England if they are to achieve success in the Champion's League, by prioritising Europe over domestic competitions. It may be that under-strength **Rangers** teams will compete in the League and Scottish Cups, as well as at certain critical points of the season in the Scottish Premier League itself. Would the **Rangers** manager sacrifice the domestic title for the chance of getting his team to the quarters, semis or final of the Champion's League?

"It is difficult to say. We will have to wait and see if that comes," said Advocaat. "We must realise that if a team, it doesn't matter which one, goes far in Europe, it costs you points in the domestic League. The game and the travelling takes a lot of energy out of you. It is a very demanding schedule." We all hope that Dick Advocaat's **Rangers** team has what it takes to cope with that schedule! ❏

FLIXPIX

1999/2000 SEASON REVIEW PART ONE

JULY 1999 — **Rangers**' season began early with the qualifying stages for the UEFA Champion's League starting in July. While other teams in Scotland were concentrating on pre-season training and friendlies, the Gers had to travel to Finnish champions FC Haka for an important fixture which, at this early stage of the season, could have proved very difficult. However, **Rangers** were on song right from the start and after Lorenzo Amoruso's thunderous free kick had given them the lead, new £4 million signing Michael Mols took centre stage. His first and second **Rangers** goals arrived before half time, both quality strikes, and 3-0 up at the break, the tie was virtually over. Jonatan Johansson added a fourth in the second period, while the Finnish side gained some consolation with a late goal. The only concern for Dick Advocaat was an injury to Mols which would rule him out for the visit of Kilmarnock to Ibrox just three days later.

Rangers unfurled the Scottish Premier League flag before the game against Killie in front of over 48,000 fans packed into Ibrox for the traditional opening day celebrations. It seemed that the party atmosphere had got to the players, especially after Rod Wallace's excellent finish from Giovanni van Bronckhorst's chip had put the Blues 1-0 up at the break. Killie had drawn 1-1 at Ibrox in the last game of the previous season and were putting up a strong fight here, even though with better finishing **Rangers** should have stretched their lead long before Ally Mitchell was allowed too much space in the box and levelled the game with a smart shot past Stefan Klos. Two years previously Mitchell had scored in the same goal to end **Rangers**' dream of winning ten titles in a row and it seemed that he would again be the Ibrox party pooper. However, just three minutes later, Claudio Reyna accepted a →

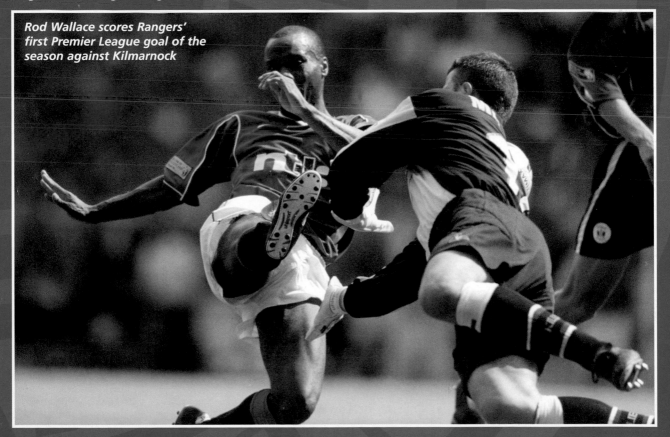

Rod Wallace scores Rangers' first Premier League goal of the season against Kilmarnock

→ pass from Jorg Albertz on the edge of the box and crashed a right-foot shot into the corner to send the fans home happy with three points on the board even before August had begun.

AUGUST 1999 — The first game of August saw FC Haka travel to Ibrox for the formality of the Second Leg of the Champion's League qualifier. Goals from Wallace, Jonatan Johansson and Gabriel Amato made the aggregate score an impressive 7-1 and earned **Rangers** a tricky Third Qualifying Round tie against Italian side Parma who had knocked them out of the UEFA Cup the previous year on their way to lifting the trophy. Before this game though, there was the potentially tricky visit to Tynecastle and it was the fantastic early season form of Mols and Reyna which saw **Rangers** cruise to a 4-0 victory over Hearts. Reyna scored the first and Mols added the second before half time, driving the ball ferociously past Gilles Rousset from a seemingly impossible angle. In the second half Albertz struck the third from just outside the penalty area and Reyna grabbed his second and **Rangers**' fourth when he headed home a Wallace cross. Bring on Parma!

In the meeting of the two teams in last season's UEFA Cup, **Rangers**' Sergio Porrini had been sent off, but this time it was Parma who had a man dismissed. Fabio Cannavaro received his marching orders in the first period after dragging Rod Wallace down, his second bookable offence. Before this, both

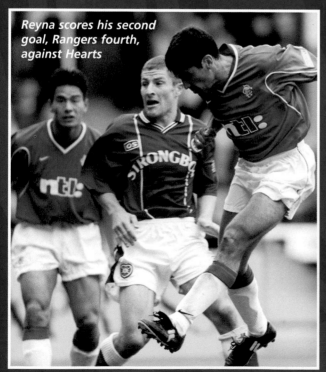

Reyna scores his second goal, Rangers fourth, against Hearts

sides had good chances to open their accounts with **Rangers** dominating possession and Parma dangerous on the counter attack. The sending off had a dramatic effect on the match and soon after Tony Vidmar's goal-bound shot was deflected by Lilian Thuram past Gianluca Buffon in the Parma goal. 1-0 up at the interval, Advocaat knew that his team had to prevent Parma scoring an away goal and attempt to get a second themselves. There were fewer chances in the second 45 minutes, though some good tracking back by Van Bronckhorst prevented Marco di Vaio converting Paolo Vanoli's pull back. **Rangers** continued to defend well against a spirited Parma fightback and on a counter attack of their own, Neil McCann threaded the ball to Reyna who fired it through a crowd of players into the back of the net. Rangers could, and maybe should, have added to the scoreline before the end but at 2-0 up the job was definitely half done.

Before the second leg in Italy, **Rangers** had to negotiate two Premier League fixtures at Ibrox, against Motherwell and Dundee United, and won both convincingly 4-1. The game with Motherwell started sluggishly as **Rangers** seemed to be suffering from their European exertions in midweek. With the scoresheet blank and with just five minutes till half time, the visitors seemed to be holding their own. However, they hadn't banked on the Michael Mols show. On 41 minutes he ruthlessly despatched Neil McCann's diagonal cross past former **Rangers** hero Andy Goram to open the scoring and on the stroke of half time slotted home McCann's centre for his second. Mols' hat trick duly arrived when he ran from the halfway line and finished expertly as Goram tried to narrow the angle with 20 minutes remaining and ten minutes later he grabbed his and **Rangers**' fourth with another quality finish. Lee McCulloch scored a last-minute consolation goal for Motherwell but this was Mols' day.

Having defeated Celtic 2-1 the previous week and with relatively good results against **Rangers** last season, including a rare victory at Ibrox, Dundee United were the perfect opposition to test **Rangers** before the game with Parma four days later. It must have been very satisfying for Advocaat as his team ran out 4-1 victors although it did take some time for them to impose themselves on Paul Sturrock's men. Reyna's exquisite 22nd minute free kick was added to by Van Bronckhorst, Wallace and Vidmar in the second half while De Vos was allowed yet another late

consolation for the opposition as the Champions dozed off towards the end.

With seven wins on the spin in all competitions from the start of the campaign, **Rangers** arrived at Parma's Ennio Tardini stadium confident that they could hold the Italian team. And so it proved, though at times things looked decidedly dodgy and Lionel Charbonnier had a fantastic match in the **Rangers** goal. Advocaat deployed a 3-5-2 system and detailed Barry Ferguson as a man marker on Ariel Ortega. With the scoresheet blank after an hour of play, Parma were beginning to become frustrated as Advocaat's game plan stifled their creativity. In fact, **Rangers** were producing some good chances of their own – Wallace headed wide and Vidmar struck the woodwork with a crashing drive. With 22 minutes remaining, Charbonnier made a rare mistake which allowed Johan Walem to score the only goal of the game. Parma surged forward for the goal which would signal extra time but **Rangers** held firm and booked their place in the Champion's League group stages.

The last game of August was at Hibernian's Easter Road and despite Sergio Porrini and Rod Wallace being absent through injury, **Rangers** took all three points. But it was not easy. Hibs' Shaun Dennis should have scored before the break but his shot cannoned off the face of the bar when he was presented with an unguarded net and Johansson cleared off the line late on following Pat McGinlay's header from Latapy's corner. In between these efforts, Johansson scored the only goal of the game when he broke Hibs' offside trap to slot home under the body of Ollie Gottskalksson. The Finnish striker made the most of his rare appearance in the first team and looked sharp throughout.

SEPTEMBER 1999 — With the group stages of the Champion's League just around the corner, Aberdeen, the whipping boys of the Scottish Premier League, arrived at Ibrox to face a **Rangers** team refreshed after a two week break enforced by international matches. The Dons had suffered 8 successive league defeats before this game and when Mols opened the scoring on 16 minutes after Amato's delightful flick, the result was never in doubt. Mols scored his second two minutes into the second half following some good work by Amato and when the Argentinian was felled in the box with five minutes left, Albertz stepped up to make the

final score 3-0. Amato was outstanding in this match and with Rod Wallace absent with hamstring problems, Advocaat must have been glad he hadn't been persuaded to part with the striker when a host of Spanish clubs showed interest in the summer.

Rangers travelled to Valencia for their first group match in the Champion's League and departed with a disappointing 2-0 reverse. The Spaniards were in scintillating form from the start and could have been well clear before the half hour mark. However, **Rangers** weathered this early storm and began to

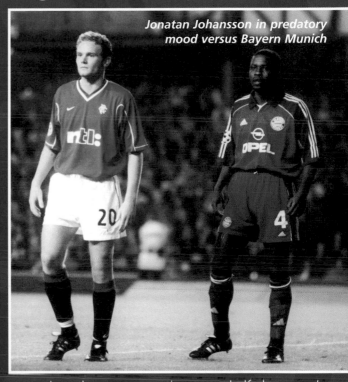

Jonatan Johansson in predatory mood versus Bayern Munich

come into the game, creating some half-chances of their own. However, a mistake by the previously inspired Charbonnier in goal saw Juan Sanchez's shot squirm towards the line and in trying to clear the ball, Craig Moore inadvertantly put the ball in his own net. Kily Gonzalez grabbed Valencia's second with 14 minutes remaining after he exchanged passes with Sanchez, but it was the lack of penetration up front which must have worried Advocaat with Bayern Munich and PSV Eindhoven to come.

A week later, the mighty Bayern Munich, who had been floored in last season's Champion's League final by Manchester United's late-late show, produced a late-late show of their own to deny **Rangers** a famous and much-needed victory. Halfway through the first half Jorg Albertz shot **Rangers** into the lead, sending the Ibrox faithful delirious. The Blues →

→ pushed forward relentlessly for the rest of the match and carved out some great chances to take the game away from the German side. However, a combination of wayward finishing and superb goalkeeping from debutant 20-year old Stefan Wessels in the Munich goal meant that the score was still only 1-0 as the game reached 90 minutes. Then Michael Tarnat drove a free kick against Arthur Numan in the **Rangers** wall and the ball deflected past Charbonnier to leave Advocaat rueing his team's wastefulness in front of goal. Back to Premier League action at home to St Johnstone four days later, Dick Advocaat gave some of his players a rest to allow as much preparation as possible for the trip to PSV Eindhoven the following week. Colin Hendry, Andrei Kanchelskis and Darius Adamczuk came in for Porrini, Amoruso and Reyna, although it was Barry Ferguson who damaged a hamstring in this match who may have wished he was rested instead. Albertz scored two goals, one a penalty and the other a trademark 'hammer' shot, and Mols added a third late on. Although Miguel Simao made the score 2-1 for a while with a powerful header, **Rangers** comfortably saw off the St Johnstone challenge.

Next was the must win game in Holland with PSV Eindhoven. With only one point from the opening two games, **Rangers** chances of progression to the second stage of the Champion's League hung by a thread. Before the game there was some good news as Ferguson passed a late fitness test. Both sides created chances in the early exchanges though neither goalkeeper was seriously tested, although when Reyna was replaced by Albertz at the mid point of the first half **Rangers** began to exert some pressure on the Eindhoven defence. McCann, Albertz and Mols had good efforts before the break and just after the interval both Luc Nilis and Ruud Van Nistelrooy should have put PSV ahead. As chances came and went from McCann and Wallace and Albertz's 25-yard drive was tipped over by PSV keeper Ronald Waterreus, it seemed that the game was destined to finish goalless. However, with just six minutes left, Albertz volleyed the winner much to Advocaat's delight to put **Rangers'** European adventure back on track.

OCTOBER 1999 — As the Premier League game at Dundee on the second day of October approached the interval with Rangers 1-0 thanks to Kanchelskis, it seemed as if a regulation victory at half pace was assured for the men in blue. However, crunching tackles from Dundee's Lee Wilkie on Barry Ferguson and Van Bronckhorst in quick succession sparked off a melée which saw both Wilkie and Van Bronckhorst red-carded and James Grady of Dundee and Numan lucky to only see yellow. The game livened up considerably in the second period and when Shaun McSkimming and then Willie Falconer scored to put Dundee in front, it seemed as if **Rangers** unbeaten Premier League record would go. Then Falconer missed an easy chance to put the game beyond **Rangers'** and when Wallace accepted Mols square ball to level the score it seemed only a matter of time before **Rangers** regained the lead. With just five minutes to go, Amato headed home Albertz's corner and normal service was resumed. Ten days later, an under-strength **Rangers** side, including young goalkeeper Mark Brown making his first team debut, made hard work of defeating Second Division Dunfermline in the CIS Insurance Cup. Rod Wallace's 25th minute finish the only goal of a fairly drab encounter.

Rangers dropped the first points of the campaign at Kilmarnock in the next game, a 1-1 draw which ended the Premier League's best ever start of eight straight wins. **Rangers** never really got out of first gear in this game despite welcoming back Stefan Klos in goal after nearly two months out and being able to field a nearly full-strength side. A scrappy start was enlivened by Van Bronckhorst's delightful chip over the Killie goalkeeper after 25 minutes and although Jerome Vareille and ex-**Rangers** star Ally McCoist went close for Kilmarnock, it remained 1-0 until 73 minutes. Then the two Kilmarnock substitutes, Christophe Cocard and Michael Jeffreys, combined with Jeffreys heading home the equaliser past Klos. **Rangers** threatened for the winner but had to be content with just one point for the first time this season.

In complete contrast was **Rangers'** performance four days later when PSV Eindhoven came to Ibrox – the home team played in top gear all night as they brushed aside the Dutch challenge with some exhilarating attacking football. Right from the start **Rangers** out-fought and out-played PSV and really should have scored more than Amoruso's bullet header and Mols' calm headed finish from McCann's centre before Van Nistelrooy halved the deficit with a penalty just before the break. At 2-1 the game may have seemed in the balance but **Rangers** were not

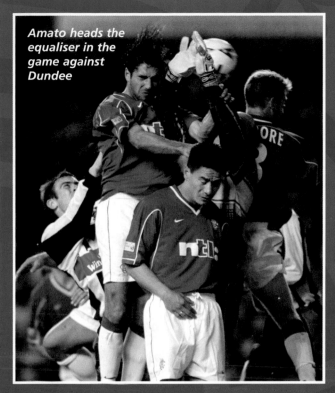

Amato heads the equaliser in the game against Dundee

going to let their fantastic play in the first half go unrewarded and within 10 minutes of the restart, McCann's close range shot had re-established the two goal cushion. There were many more chances, as well as at least two penalty appeals, before Mols wrapped up the points with an emphatic finish following his run from the halfway line. **Rangers** biggest crowd of the season, 50,083, had witnessed one of the team's best ever performances on the European stage, but there was still a lot of work to do!

Another crowd exceeding 50,000 arrived at Ibrox on 26 October for the visit of Valencia, knowing that a win would guarantee **Rangers'** passage into the uncharted waters of the second phase of the Champion's League. However, by half time, Valencia were already two goals up through Mendieta and Claudio Lopez and despite a close-range strike from Craig Moore after an hour it was Valencia and not **Rangers** who had guaranteed progression in the competition. Valencia were good value for their victory overall and although Jorg Albertz nearly grabbed an equaliser when he fired inches wide of the far post in the closing moments, it was clear that however far **Rangers** had come in this season, there was still a lot of work for Dick Advocaat to do.

Qualification now rested on the last game of the group – against Bayern Munich in the Olympic Stadium in a week's time. Before that showdown, **Rangers** registered their biggest ever Premier Division defeat of Aberdeen with a 5-1 mauling which

was probably not quite as emphatic as the scoreline suggests. Aberdeen's Paul Bernard was sent off in the first period for a late tackle on Giovanni van Bronckhorst and by the break **Rangers** were beginning to turn the screw, although it wasn't until the 67th and 69th minute that Mols and Amato put the game beyond the Dons – to answer Aberdeen's 10th minute penalty from Solberg and Johansson's first on 23 minutes. Before the end, Johansson completed his hat trick with a couple of smart finishes to stake his claim for a starting place in the Munich decider, having come on as a substitute in the Valencia defeat.

NOVEMBER 1999 — The final match of the Champion's League was the first hurdle for **Rangers** to overcome in November and it was win or bust in Munich. **Rangers** set about Bayern Munich with a determination and skill equal to that shown against Parma at Ibrox. Bayern won and qualified for the next stage, but **Rangers** could take heart from this game knowing that they ran last season's finalists very close and were only defeated by a controversial first-half penalty. By the end of the game, Bayern were very, very relieved to hear the final whistle. Tragically for **Rangers** they lost Michael Mols when he raced for a loose ball with Bayern Munich goalkeeper Oliver Khan and caused severe damage to his knee ligaments. Mols was later ruled out for the remainder of the season and the sneaking suspicion was that if he had stayed on the pitch, **Rangers** could very well have won this game. Without him, all the **Rangers** pressure and possession came to nothing and the front duo of Rod Wallace and Jonatan Johansson could not get that vital goal. Still it was a performance to be proud of and though well short of completion, demonstrated the Dick Advocaat revolution.

There was no time for **Rangers** to hide their disappointment with Celtic visiting Ibrox the following Sunday in the first League meeting of the Old Firm pair. **Rangers** took the lead early on through Johansson, but Celtic scored twice through Eyal Berkovic before **Rangers** were awarded a controversial penalty on the stroke of half time. Jorg Albertz was in the penalty area about to cross the ball when Paolo Lamberto came crashing in with a two-footed lunge, injuring himself in the process. **Rangers** were awarded the penalty but Lamberto was lucky not to be red carded even though he was →

→ carried off with facial injuries. **Rangers** stepped up the pressure in the second half and Lorenzo Amoruso scored with a rasping free kick before Amato showed great skill and trickery to seal a 4-2 win. A regulation win at Ibrox over Hibs followed – Johansson and Albertz scoring in a 2-0 victory – before another big European tie against Borussia Dortmund loomed at Ibrox in the UEFA Cup. **Rangers** were without a goalkeeper, both Klos and Charbonnier were on the treatment table, and borrowed Thomas Myhre from Everton for a month. Amoruso was also missing but Craig Moore and Tony Vidmar proved excellent in the centre of defence. Although Bobic headed two good efforts wide when he might well have scored for the Germans, **Rangers** were good value overall for the 2-0 win. The highlight of the game was Rod Wallace's goal just prior to the interval which came after a slick build-up. The other goal was an 18th minute og from the experienced Jürgen Kohler. The only nagging doubt for **Rangers** fans was that two goals is never enough with the away tie at Dortmund to come.

The last game of the month saw a shock home defeat against Dundee, ending **Rangers'** unbeaten Premier League record. Dundee took the lead through Craig Ireland after 14 minutes, although **Rangers** equalised with twenty minutes remaining when Rod Wallace tapped home after Neil McCann's header had come back off a post. Albertz had already missed a 53rd minute penalty, Dundee keeper Robert Douglas parrying a fairly weak effort, and it looked as though both teams would have to settle for a point as the rain lashed down. However, deep into injury time Gavin Rae took the ball on his chest and finished superbly to win the game 2-1 for the visitors. The consolation for **Rangers** was that later on the same day, Celtic managed to lose 3-2 to Motherwell to preserve the lead at the top of the table.

DECEMBER 1999 — December started badly for **Rangers** and for a time it looked as though the whole season was beginning to come off the rails. Firstly, a weakened **Rangers** team minus nine First Team regulars went to Aberdeen for a CIS League Cup tie. With the game goalless after ninety minutes, and with only three minutes of extra time remaining, penalties seemed inevitable. However, Andy Dow popped up to win the game for the team rooted to the bottom of the Premier League and **Rangers** were out of the competition they had won the previous year. Of course, Dick Advocaat was looking to more

Neil McCann lifts the ball over the oncoming Hibernian keeper

important games so the loss wasn't too great, but with the first league defeat of the season in the last game and with the all-important away match at Borussia Dortmund, it wasn't good for morale to miss out on a trip to Hampden later in the season.

Next up was the return game against Dortmund with **Rangers** leading 2-0 from the first leg and after that sparkling display at Ibrox, hopes were high that a passage to the next round could be gained. However, like the away games against Parma and Valencia, **Rangers** sat too deep allowing Dortmund to attack continuously throughout the first period. Just as it looked like **Rangers** were going to go in 0-0 at half time, Dortmund scored. Victor Ikpeba scored for the Germans direct from a corner as he was left unmarked on the far post. The second half was extremely tense and nerve-racking as Dortmund piled forward in increasingly desperate waves, although both McCann and Reyna had chances for **Rangers** which would have put the tie out of the home side's reach. As the

FLIXPIX

Billy Dodds had been signed for £1.4 million from Dundee United and made his debut in this game. Dodds has always been a hardworking goalscorer and Dick Advocaat was keen to get him straight into First Team action with Rod Wallace struggling with injury and loss of form. **Rangers** next visited Motherwell's Fir Park with both Dodds and Kanchelskis notching two goals in an emphatic 5-1 victory. Motherwell contributed fully to a sparkling game in which **Rangers** seemed to be approaching the excellent form of earlier in the season, particularly Kanchelskis who scored the first and fifth goals and had a hand in both of Dodds' strikes, and Ferguson who was excellent throughout. The other scorer was Amoruso, who struck a ferocious free kick in the 34th minute.

Next was the visit of Hearts to Ibrox in an SPL match which coincided with the celebration of 100 years of Ibrox. There were plenty of famous "old faces" on show and a carnival atmosphere but sadly the game failed to live up to the show. **Rangers** won thanks to a late strike from Jorg Albertz. Hearts had come to defend and former **Rangers** keeper, Anttii Niemi, was kept busy although Advocaat would have liked to have seen him more tested than he was. Chances came and went for Dodds, Wallace, Kanchelskis and Amoruso before "The Hammer" struck to take **Rangers** four points clear of Celtic at the top of the table. The final game of 1999 was the visit to Celtic who had been in good form lately, rattling in goals, with Viduka in particular the star man. However, despite scoring early on through Viduka, Celtic didn't have it all their own way and Rangers soon equalised through Billy Dodds. Gradually **Rangers** came more and more into the game and although this game was as passionate as any Old Firm game, it never threatened to boil over in the same way as the corresponding fixture the previous season. So the first ever winter break began and **Rangers** went to Florida for some training and rest. The team started off very well this season and got off to a flier by beating Parma, but once Mols was injured, a certain edge was taken off the performances. Rod Wallace had been unable to shake off a hamstring injury and had not been able to reproduce his excellent form of last season. The break would undoubtedly do the players good, allow injuries to heal and more importantly allow them to recoup mentally.

game moved into injury time at the end of the game, **Rangers** fans could almost sense the prospect of European football in spring. Then Dortmund goalkeeper Lehmann ventured into the **Rangers** penalty area and when the ball wasn't cleared properly, his mis-kick fell kindly to Bobic who finished clinically to take the game into extra time. **Rangers** did have a couple of chances to win the game in extra time but with both sets of players obviously tired, penalty kicks were almost inevitable. Dortmund won easily in the end with Giovanni van Bronckhorst, Arthur Numan and Claudio Reyna missing from the spot, and in heartbreaking fashion **Rangers** were out of Europe. Now they had to concentrate on domestic action.

There were four Premier League games before the innovative winter break and first up was a dreary game against Kilmarnock which took an Albertz goal after 56 minutes to win with no sign of any improvements in **Rangers** form. On the bright side,

SEASON REVIEW CONTINUED ON PAGE 36

JORG ALBERTZ

Height: 1.87m
Weight: 86kg
Date of Birth: 29/01/71
Place of Birth: Monchengladbach (Germany)
Signed From: HSV Hamburg in July 1996
for £4 million
Previous Clubs: Borussia Monchengladbach,
Fortuna Dusseldorf and HSV Hamburg
Position: Midfield
Squad Number: 11
International Caps: 3 – Germany

Jorg Albertz was signed by Walter Smith, the then **Rangers** manager, from German Bundesliga side Hamburg for £4 million in the summer of 1996. Jorg had spent his formative years at his home town club Borussia Monchengladbach before joining Fortuna Dusseldorf in the German second division. After three seasons in Dusseldorf, scoring four goals in 58 League games, he made the move to Hamburg. He made 99 league appearances for Hamburg in three years and also became club captain. Albertz was beginning to earn a reputation as a goal-scoring midfielder – in his time at Hamburg he notched up 22 goals, many of them spectacular efforts from outside the penalty area. He gained his nickname "The Hammer" during this time. When his shooting was measured with a speed gun it was found to be in the region of 80 miles per hour! In the season before he joined Rangers, Jorg helped Hamburg to European qualification by reaching 5th place in the Bundesliga.

Once at Ibrox, Albertz settled comfortably into a left-sided midfield

JORG ALBERTZ

FLIXPIX

THE HAMMER

role. He soon endeared himself to the fans with his fantastic performances and outrageous goals, many from long range free-kicks, including a magnificent effort in the Old Firm game with Celtic. He also demonstrated his enormous pride in playing for the Gers, often kissing the badge on his shirt during goalscoring celebrations. Publicly he has also stated his love for the Glasgow club and his admiration for the never-say-die attitude of the Scottish players which, he says, breeds exciting football.

During both of his first two years at Ibrox his goal tally reached double figures. In the 1998/99 season, Albertz grabbed the winning goal in the League Cup Final as **Rangers** beat St Johnstone 2-1 and he scored his first hat-trick for the Club in the 6-1 League victory over Dundee at Ibrox in February 1999. He continued his good form throughout the season and finished second in the Ibrox scoring charts with 19 goals in 50 appearances. His return of goals from midfield has made him a very valuable player in Dick Advocaat's Ibrox revolution.

At the start of the 1999-2000 season, Jorg was one of the few Ibrox players who could have considered themselves automatic starters in the first team and his early season form was rewarded with four Scottish Premier League goals by the end of September. He transferred his domestic form into European competition, scoring against Bayern Munich at Ibrox and grabbing the vital winner against PSV in Eindhoven. By the time Scottish football paused for its first ever winter break, Albertz had demonstrated exactly how vital he was to Advocaat's team by performing heroically in games where the team as a whole had been a little lacklustre. He scored the only goals of the game in the two home Scottish Premier League fixtures with Kilmarnock and Hearts in December to help keep **Rangers** top of the Premier League into 2000. In the new year, Albertz continued to be a rock in the **Rangers** midfield as the Blues cruised to the Premier League and Scottish Cup double, but probably his most satisfying game was the 4-0 drubbing of Celtic in the last Old Firm game of the season. He opened the scoring after only four minutes with a close range effort and grabbed his second late on with a spectacular overhead kick. This win virtually guaranteed **Rangers** the title and the celebrations which followed showed just how much this win meant to Albertz and his teammates.

Towards the end of the year, there was much speculation in the press about Jorg leaving Ibrox, but just before the Scottish Cup Final he signed a new three-year deal, pledging his future to **Rangers** and manager Dick Advocaat. It had been well documented that before the season began, while Jorg was a firm favourite with the fans, he had yet to completely win over Advocaat. His outstanding displays and 20 goals were proof enough to the management at Ibrox that he was well worth further investment.

As Albertz said: "I am delighted to continue my career at **Rangers** and demonstrate my commitment to the club by signing this new deal. It was never in my plans or my intention to leave this great club and I look forward to many more successful seasons." Amen to that! ❏

DID YOU KNOW? - Jorg Albertz was the first ever Rangers player to be capped by Germany when he played against Romania in September 1998.

---

welcome to
IBROX

Ibrox Stadium, home of Rangers Football Club, is one of the leading sports grounds in the world and is one of only 12 in Europe awarded 5-star status by UEFA. Let's take a closer look:

1. JUMBOTRONS
Situated at the northern corners of the stadium, the two massive Jumbotron television screens show pre-match entertainment, live pictures during the game and also beam back coverage of away games.

2. ALL-SEATER STANDS
When the top tier was added to the Main Stand in 1991, Ibrox became a completely enclosed stadium with 50,500 seats. However, there are also plush executive suites, conference rooms and a superb restaurant which is open to the public.

3. THE PITCH
Measuring 115 by 78 yards, this lush stretch of turf is the focus for the unrivalled

passion of the loyal Rangers supporters all over the world.

4. RANGERS SHOP
The Club Superstore supplies fans with a wide range of official Rangers merchandise, from badges to backpacks to babies' bibs.

5. TROPHY ROOM
Opened in 1959, the Rangers Trophy Room is crammed full of display cabinets featuring vast quantities of silverware, porcelain, crystal and medals. There's even a racing cycle presented to Rangers by the French Club Saint-Etienne when the clubs met in the 1975 European Cup.

6. RECEPTION/STAIRCASE
Enter the front door of Ibrox Stadium and

be impressed by the air of tradition and excellence. Walk up the famous marble staircase and remember the great names of the past who once called Ibrox home.

7. MANAGER'S OFFICE

At the top of the marble staircase is the Manager's Office, where Dick Advocaat, like those famous managers of the past, plans Rangers' conquests.

8. BOARD ROOM

It is here in the Rangers Board Room that David Murray and his Directors meet to decide on the future of Rangers Football Club – and, of course, whether to make that big money signing!

9. DRESSING ROOMS

In the dressing rooms, the shirts bear the names of star players from all over the world and it is here that Dick Advocaat gives his men the final instructions before they take the field.

VAN BRONCKHORST

GIOVANNI VAN BRONCKHORST

Height: 1.76m — **Weight:** 72.7kg
Date of Birth: 05/02/75
Place of Birth: Rotterdam (Holland)
Signed From: Feyenoord in July 1998
for £5.25 million
Previous Club: Feyenoord
Position: Midfield
Squad Number: 8
International Caps: 20 – Holland

Giovanni van Bronckhorst joined **Rangers** after the World Cup in France in 1998 where his Dutch team reached the semi-finals. Although he didn't make much impact at that tournament, he soon imposed himself on Scottish football and by the end of his first year at Ibrox the promise he had shown as a young player at Feyenoord had come to fruition.

After he scored on his debut in the 5-3 UEFA Cup victory over Shelbourne, playing in a left-back role, he switched into the midfield and remained there for the rest of the campaign. By the end of his first season, he had scored a total of nine goals, including **Rangers**' first against Bayer Leverkusen in Germany.

The 1999/2000 season was a good one for Giovanni, his six goals including **Rangers**' fourth at Ibrox in the 4-0 hammering of Celtic and one of the four against Aberdeen in the Scottish Cup Final which captured the double. He was also close to winning the Football Writers' Player of the Year award, pipped to the title by teammate Barry Ferguson.

Giovanni is a wonderfully gifted midfield player who shows great touch and vision when on the ball and is also prepared to work hard when not in possession. He is still only 25, at the peak of his physical fitness, and with the experience gained with Holland at Euro 2000 behind him, watch out for some more commanding performances from Giovanni in the **Rangers** midfield this year! ❑

FLIXPIX

BILLY DODDS

When Dick Advocaat was faced with long-term injuries to Michael Mols, Jonatan Johansson and Gabriel Amato just before Christmas 1999, he swooped for Billy Dodds from Dundee United in a deal worth £1.3 million to help ease his striker crisis.

Dodds is one of the best natural goalscorers in British football. He possesses good acceleration, a quick turn of pace and for someone who is only five foot eight, he is surprisingly strong in the air. He is also a very willing worker who displays great commitment.

His career began as a 17-year old at Chelsea before moving back to Scotland, initially on loan with Partick Thistle. In his first start for Dundee United in September 1998, after his move from Aberdeen, he grabbed a hat trick against St Johnstone and went on to score 27 goals in his 54 games for the Tannadice side.

Dodds made his debut for Scotland in Estonia at the age of 29 and now looks like a regular in the international team.

His impact at Ibrox was immediate as he grabbed two goals in the 5-1 win over Motherwell on 18 December and then went on to score in his Old Firm debut nine days later. By the time he scored in the Scottish Cup Final against Aberdeen, he had notched up 15 goals in 17 games.

The 2000/2001 season has also started well for Dodds – he grabbed both **Rangers'** goals in the opening day 2-1 victory over St Johnstone. ❑

BILLY DODDS

Height: 1.73m — Weight: 79kg
Date of Birth: 05/02/69
Place of Birth: New Cumnock
Signed From: Dundee United in December 1999 for £1.3 million
Previous Clubs: Chelsea, Dundee, St Johnstone, Aberdeen, Dundee United
Position: Forward — Squad Number: 16
International Caps: 19 – Scotland

BARRY FERGUSON

BARRY FERGUSON

Height: 1.80m
Weight: 74kg
Date of Birth: 02/02/78
Place of Birth: Glasgow
Signed From: Product of Ibrox Youth Policy
Previous Clubs: None
Position: Midfield
Squad Number: 6
International Caps: 7 – Scotland

Barry Ferguson is the younger brother of former **Rangers** favourite Derek and first came to Ibrox as a 16 year old schoolboy. He has progressed rapidly through the schoolboy and reserve teams at Ibrox and from the moment he was voted man of the match on his debut against Hearts in the last game of the 1996/97 season, he has earned rave reviews for his commanding midfield displays.

In Walter Smith's last year at Ibrox, Ferguson forced his way into the First Team squad, ending the year with seven appearances to his name. When Dick Advocaat took over as manager, he saw in the young Scot a central midfielder of great promise and he has regularly started Ferguson amongst the wealth of foreign stars at Ibrox. To Ferguson's credit, with every passing game he has rapidly developed and matured and he is now widely regarded as the hottest property in Scottish football. So much so, that he has begun to attract interest from clubs abroad, although in October 1999 he signed an extended 6-year contract which will keep him at Ibrox until 2005.

Barry Ferguson is also a full Scottish international, having made his debut in the Euro 2000 qualifier against Lithuania.

Last season, Ferguson won the Football Writers' Player of the Year award and made the most appearances of any Rangers player – 49! This season we all hope Barry will further enhance his reputation abroad with his performances in Europe! ❑

FLIXPIX

MICHAEL MOLS

Highly rated Dutch international striker Michael Mols joined **Rangers** in the summer of 1999 for £4 million from FC Utrecht, turning down a move to the English Premier League with Sheffield Wednesday. The 28-year-old was in sparkling form as soon as arrived, scoring twice on his debut against FC Haka in the Champion's League qualifier and then grabbing all four goals in the 4-1 victory over Motherwell in only his second start.

Mols went on to score a total of 9 Scottish Premier League goals in only 9 starts, as well as a double strike in **Rangers'** fantastic 4-1 Champion's League victory away at PSV Eindhoven. Unfortunately, Michael's season was cut short when he sustained a serious knee ligament injury in the last Champion's League game with Bayern Munich which put an end to his first season at Ibrox.

Mols' career began at Ajax when he was only 15. He went on to join Cambuur Leeuwarden before moving to FC Utrecht where he was a firm crowd favourite. When his transfer to Rangers was imminent, the Utrecht fans organised a petition, desperate for the striker to stay.

Mols is a prolific goalscorer with bags of skill. One of his greatest assets is his ability to turn defenders and leave them for dead with blistering pace. He can then advance on goal to finish with composure. Hopefully he will quickly get over his injury problems and be back to his very best this season. ❏

MICHAEL MOLS

Height: 1.79m — Weight: 78.7kg
Date of Birth: 17/12/70
Place of Birth: Amsterdam (Holland)
Signed From: FC Utrecht in March 1999 for £4 million
Previous Clubs: Cambuur Leeuwarden, FC Utrecht
Position: Forward — Squad Number: 9
International Caps: 1 – Holland

THE
OLD FIRM

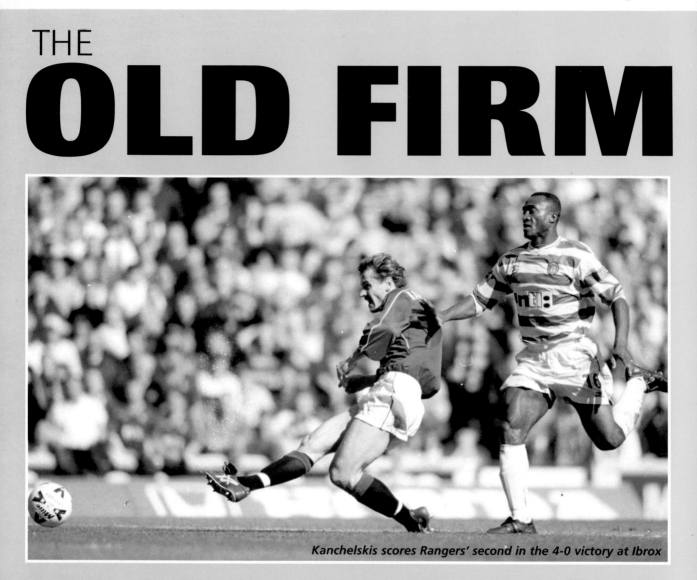

Kanchelskis scores Rangers' second in the 4-0 victory at Ibrox

Wallace wins the game late on with the only goal in the derby on 8 March

DERBY

RANGERS VS CELTIC RESULTS 1999/2000

Sun 7 November 1999	**Rangers** Johansson (19) Albertz (pen 45) Amoruso (49) Amato (66)	4 - 2	Celtic Berkovic (21, 42)
Mon 27 December 1999	Celtic Viduka (18)	1 - 1	**Rangers** Dodds (27)
Wed 8 March 2000	Celtic	0 - 1	**Rangers** Wallace (86)
Sun 26 March 2000	**Rangers** Albertz (4, 84) Kanchelskis (41) Van Bronckhorst (87)	4 - 0	Celtic

Albertz scores the first of his two goals on 26 March

SCOTTISH PREMIER LEAGUE
WORDSEARCH

In the grid below are eleven of this year's Scottish Premier League teams. See if you can find them all and try to identify which one is missing. Also, there is a First Division team hiding in the grid. Which one? The answers are on Page 64.

E	N	I	L	M	R	E	F	N	U	D
K	C	H	J	N	B	D	E	R	R	E
S	I	H	I	B	E	R	N	I	A	N
T	T	L	H	E	A	R	T	S	N	O
M	L	Q	M	W	B	P	O	K	F	T
I	E	S	F	A	E	L	H	R	A	S
R	C	C	V	B	R	J	D	Y	L	N
R	J	U	I	M	D	N	Z	S	K	H
E	D	U	N	D	E	E	O	Z	I	O
N	R	A	N	G	E	R	S	C	R	J
Y	T	B	N	S	N	U	I	B	K	T
L	L	E	W	R	E	H	T	O	M	S

FLIXPIX

SPOT the BALL

We have removed the football from the picture below. Take a close look and use your football skill to judge where the centre of the ball should be. Then use the grid to get a co-ordinate for the square the ball has been removed from (for example: A1). Check your answer on Page 64!

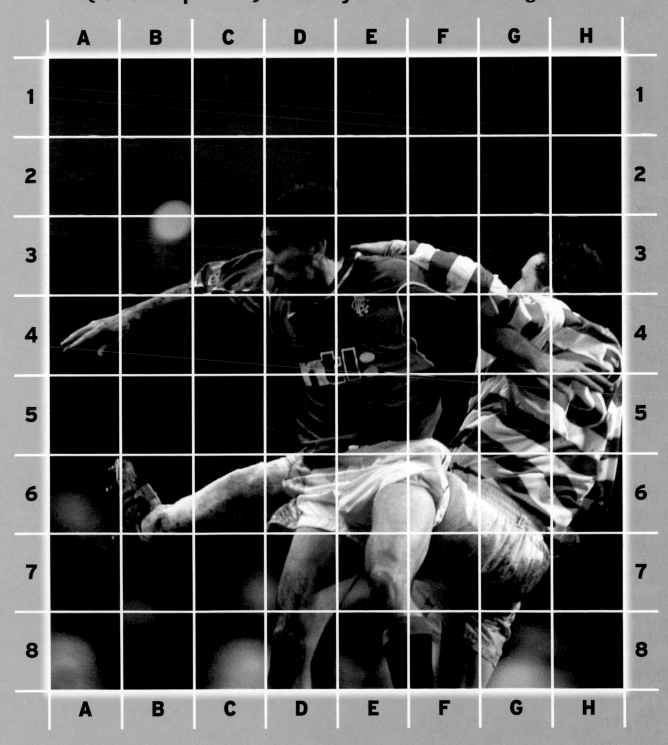

ANDREI KANCHELSKIS

ANDREI KANCHELSKIS

Height: 1.80m — **Weight:** 84kg
Date of Birth: 23/01/69
Place of Birth: Kirovograd (Ukraine)
Signed from: Fiorentina in July 1998
for £5.5 million
Previous Clubs: Shaktor Donetsk,
Manchester United, Everton, Fiorentina
Position: Midfield — **Squad Number:** 7
International Caps: 60 – Ukraine/Soviet Union

Andrei Kanchelskis became **Rangers'** record signing when the pacy midfielder was bought for £5.5 million from Italian side Fiorentina in July 1998. He played local football until he was spotted by Dinamo Kiev. He spent most of his time in the reserves, however, and in 1988 joined Shakhtyor Donetsk, the team he had supported as a boy.

Within a year he had been capped by the Soviet Union, coming on as a substitute against Poland in August 1989. He was signed by Alex Ferguson at Manchester United for £650,000 in March 1991. He won two Premier League titles with United, in 1992-93 and 1993-94, and was part of the latter season's Double-winning victory. He also won the League Cup when United beat Nottingham Forest 1-0 in 1992.

Kanchelskis finished the 1994-95 season as United's top scorer with 15 goals. But after a dispute with the club, was sold to Everton for £5 million in August 1995. He scored 16 goals in his first season at Goodison prompting Fiorentina to pay £8 million in January 1997.

Andrei made his **Rangers** debut in the 2-0 UEFA Cup victory over Shelbourne at Ibrox in July 1998 and scored his first goal in the next round in the 2-0 victory over PAOK Salonika. However, an injury sustained in the Championship run-in meant he didn't figure in **Rangers** early games of the 1999-2000 season. He made his comeback in the 1-0 away at Hibs at the end of August. ❑

CRAIG MOORE

Craig Moore rejoined the club in April 1999 after a short spell at English club Crystal Palace.

Dick Advocaat had never really wanted to let Moore go, as he played his best football for **Rangers** under the Dutch coach. But with his contract reaching its end, Moore was sold to the London club before he was available to leave for free. But when Palace's financial troubles escalated they were unable to pay **Rangers** what they were owed and in an unusual move, the player returned to Ibrox.

Advocaat quickly made it clear that Moore was his first choice to partner Lorenzo Amoruso for the start of the 1999-2000 season and presented him with the number 3 shirt. Despite some shaky early performances, Moore steadied his game and has shown why Advocaat has such faith in him.

His performances in both the League and the Champion's League won him rave reviews from fans and pundits alike as he scooped a Player of the Month award in December.

He brought that form into 2000 and his commanding displays put him into contention for the Scottish Player of the Year award. He sustained a knee injury in March that kept him out for the rest of the season and although it was starting to clear up, nobody thought he would play in the Scottish Cup Final.

Dick Advocaat took a risk and pitched him into action against Aberdeen at Hampden and it paid off as **Rangers** won 4-0. ❑

CRAIG MOORE

Height: 1.85m
Weight: 80kg
Date of Birth: 12/12/75
Place of Birth: Canterbury (Australia)
Signed From: Crystal Palace in April 1999
Previous Clubs: Rangers, Crystal Palace
Position: Defender — **Squad Number:** 3
International Caps: 17 – Australia

Imagine you are Dick Advocaat and have just given your Rangers players their final team-talk and sent them onto the famous Ibrox pitch for an all-important Scottish Premier League encounter against Celtic. Now all you can do is watch and hope that your preparations will prove enough against the cream of Scottish football ... or is it? With just a little imagination and a couple of dice, you can recreate all the excitement of football with this game that you can play on your own or with a friend.

YOU WILL NEED
Two dice (preferably of different colours) and pen and paper (to keep the score!).

BEFORE YOU START
Decide which of the two dice will be Dice 1 and which will be Dice 2 – this is very important!

FOR TWO PLAYERS
If you are playing with a friend, decide who is going to kick off by tossing a coin. The winner of the toss will now be PLAYER 1, while the loser is PLAYER 2. PLAYER 1 starts and will be 'in possession of the ball'. PLAYER 1 throws both dice at the same time. When they have stopped rolling, refer to the table below to see what happened in this passage of play. If the result of the throw is 'keep possession' then PLAYER 1 should throw the dice again and play continues until the result of the throw is 'lose possession'. At this point, PLAYER 2 'takes possession of the ball' and throws the dice, following the instructions below until he loses possession.

SCORING A GOAL
When the dice are thrown and the result is a GOAL, then whoever has possession has scored a goal. Make a note on your piece of

paper of the current score and possession passes to the other player who now 'kicks-off' and play continues as before.

TIMING
There are many ways of deciding how long each game should be, you could play until your tea is ready, for example. However, probably the best way is to decide a target of, say, 5 or 10 goals, and as soon as one of you has reached this number the game is over. If you have a watch or even a stopwatch you can play for a set period of time, say 5 minutes, although you will have to be careful about time-wasting as the match draws to an end! You could also play for two halves with PLAYER 2 kicking off the second half.

FOR ONE PLAYER
In order to play on your own then you should follow the instructions for the two-player game although, of course, you will be both players at the same time and will throw the dice regardless of who is in possession. To make things a little easier and more fun, imagine that the two different PLAYERS are teams that you know (for example, Rangers and Celtic) and remember which team has possession of the ball as you play.

FLIXPIX

FOOTBALL'S A FUNNY OLD GAME!

TABLE

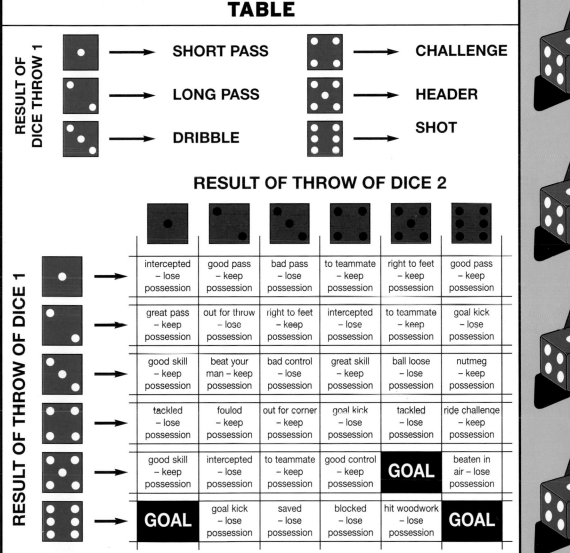

RESULT OF DICE THROW 1

- [1] → SHORT PASS
- [2] → LONG PASS
- [3] → DRIBBLE
- [4] → CHALLENGE
- [5] → HEADER
- [6] → SHOT

RESULT OF THROW OF DICE 2

RESULT OF THROW OF DICE 1

	1	2	3	4	5	6
1	intercepted – lose possession	good pass – keep possession	bad pass – lose possession	to teammate – keep possession	right to feet – keep possession	good pass – keep possession
2	great pass – keep possession	out for throw – lose possession	right to feet – keep possession	intercepted – lose possession	to teammate – keep possession	goal kick – lose possession
3	good skill – keep possession	beat your man – keep possession	bad control – lose possession	great skill – keep possession	ball loose – lose possession	nutmeg – keep possession
4	tackled – lose possession	fouled – keep possession	out for corner – keep possession	goal kick – lose possession	tackled – lose possession	ride challenge – keep possession
5	good skill – keep possession	intercepted – lose possession	to teammate – keep possession	good control – keep possession	**GOAL**	beaten in air – lose possession
6	**GOAL**	goal kick – lose possession	saved – lose possession	blocked – lose possession	hit woodwork – lose possession	**GOAL**

FOR EXAMPLE

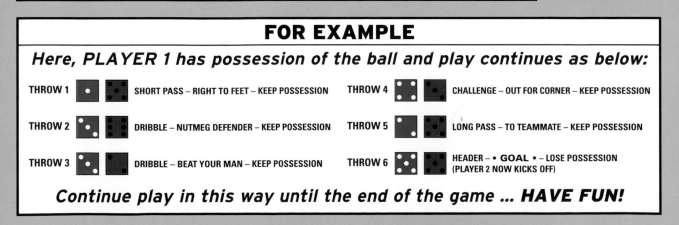

Here, PLAYER 1 has possession of the ball and play continues as below:

THROW 1 SHORT PASS – RIGHT TO FEET – KEEP POSSESSION

THROW 2 DRIBBLE – NUTMEG DEFENDER – KEEP POSSESSION

THROW 3 DRIBBLE – BEAT YOUR MAN – KEEP POSSESSION

THROW 4 CHALLENGE – OUT FOR CORNER – KEEP POSSESSION

THROW 5 LONG PASS – TO TEAMMATE – KEEP POSSESSION

THROW 6 HEADER – • **GOAL** • – LOSE POSSESSION (PLAYER 2 NOW KICKS OFF)

Continue play in this way until the end of the game ... HAVE FUN!

LORENZO AMORUSO

LORENZO AMORUSO

Height: 1.94m — **Weight:** 90kg
Date of Birth: 28/06/71
Place of Birth: Bari (Italy)
Signed From: Fiorentina in May 1997
for £4 million
Previous Clubs: Bari, Fiorentina
Position: Defender
Squad Number: 4
International Caps: None

Club captain Lorenzo Amoruso was born in Bari where he played for his local team in three different spells. In between, he had stints at Mantova and Pescavo, but it was during his third term at Bari that he established himself as a regular in the side.

He played a total of 75 League games for Bari, scoring seven goals, before joining Fiorentina for the 1995-96 season. He spent two years at Fiorentina, playing 54 games in Serie A and scoring three goals, before joining **Rangers** for £4 million in the summer preceding the 1997-98 season.

He made his debut against Celtic at Parkhead, but played only four League games as an Achilles tendon injury, which required three operations, kept him out of the game for 10 months.

Amoruso says: 'Last season was difficult because of my injury. I was always asking myself: When will I play? Will I play again? Will I be the same player as I was?' Dick Advocaat showed faith in Amoruso, however, making him captain at the start of the 1998-99 season. He lifted his first trophy when **Rangers** beat St Johnstone 2-1 in the League Cup Final on 29 November and went on to complete the treble with two superb performances against Celtic in both the League and the Scottish Cup Final.

Lorenzo can be assured of a place in history as one of the select few who have led the Ibrox club to a domestic treble. ❑

Neil McCann became Dick Advocaat's tenth signing when he joined **Rangers** from Hearts for £1.6 million in December 1998. He made his debut as a substitute in a 3-2 League victory at Tynecastle on 19 December. McCann made his international debut just three months before, also as a substitute, in a European Championship qualifier versus Lithuania.

McCann joined Dundee from Port Glasgow Boys club and made his first League appearances in the 1992-93 season. McCann was in the Dundee side that reached the League Cup Final in 1995 where they lost 2-0 to Aberdeen and at the end of that season he signed for Hearts for £200,000 in July 1996. He played 73 League games for Hearts, scoring 18 goals, and appeared in two Cup Finals for them, both against **Rangers**. The first was the 1996 League Cup Final which **Rangers** won 4-3 and the second was the 1998 Scottish Cup Final which Hearts won 2-1.

He scored his first ever goal for **Rangers** in the 6-0 rout of Hamilton in the Fourth Round of the Scottish Cup in February and went on to notch eight goals in 20 starts in the rest of the 1998/99 season. His two goals at Parkhead against Celtic on 2 May brought the title back to Ibrox.

Often used as a wide striker by Advocaat, McCann's pace frightens defenders and his crosses have delivered plenty of goals for his fellow strikers. He also grabbed four goals last season including one in the 4-1 victory over PSV. ❑

NEIL McCANN

Height: 1.75m — **Weight:** 66kg
Date of Birth: 11/08/74
Place of Birth: Greenock (Scotland)
Signed From: Hearts in December 1998 for 1.6 million
Previous Clubs: Dundee, Hearts
Position: Winger
Squad Number: 18
International Caps: 8 – Scotland

Club captain Lorenzo Amoruso enjoying the post match celebrations after their game with Dundee.

TUGAY KERIMOGLU

Height: 1.75m
Weight: 75kg
Date of Birth: 28/08/70
Place of Birth: Istanbul (Turkey)
Signed From: Galatasaray in January 2000
Previous Clubs: Galatasaray
Position: Midfield
Squad Number: 26
International Caps: 64 – Turkey

Tugay Kerimoglu became the first ever Turk to play in Scottish football when **Rangers** shelled out £1.3 million for his services.

A hero in his home country, Tugay had spent an incredible 14 years with Galatasaray and now the 29-year-old midfielder is carving out a new life in Scotland at Ibrox.

The Turkish international who has collected 64 caps for his native country decided to make the move overseas, and 'Gers had to battle against Newcastle, Benfica, Real Zaragoza and Valencia to land his signature.

But with a recommendation from former Light Blues and Galatasaray boss Graeme Souness no less, Dick Advocaat managed to persuade the highly-talented player to come to Glasgow.

Italian Marco Negri started at Italian side Cosenza in 1994. He joined **Rangers** in July 1997 for £3.75 million from Serie A side Perugia and was a sensation in his first season at the club with 36 goals.

He scored twice on his debut as **Rangers** beat Hearts 3-1 and on August 23, 1997 he scored all five goals in a 5-1 rout of Dundee United. But an eye injury sustained playing squash with teammate Sergio Porrini in January 1998 coincided with a loss of form and the goals dried up.

A £4m move to Spanish side Real Betis fell through in June that year. Negri didn't feature again for nearly two years until Advocaat called him up to the squad for a friendly against Sparta Rotterdam in January 2000.

He finally played a competitive game again in February when he appeared as a substitute in a Scottish Cup tie against Morton. But a back injury sidelined the player again until the beginning of this season. Negri has since returned to training and has played several games at under-21 level. ❑

MARCO NEGRI

Tugay said: 'I was one of the best players in the Galatasaray team but I now have to prove to myself and the rest of the world that I can be the best at another club. I know the Galatasaray fans will always love me and that is something I will always be thankful for. But I needed a new challenge. I'm not the kind of person to sit around and be happy with an easy life. I could have stayed in Turkey and wallowed in my own name but I don't want the easy life, I want to show everyone that I can succeed in Europe with **Rangers**.'

Tugay has struggled to command a regular First Team place during his first few months at Ibrox but he has been outstanding when he has been given the chance. ❑

  MARCO NEGRI

Height: 1.81m — Weight: 80.9kg
Date of Birth: 27/10/70
Place of Birth: Milan (Italy)
Signed From: Perugia in July 1997
for £3.75 million
Previous Clubs: Perugia
Position: Striker
Squad Number: 35
International Caps: None

The Official Rangers Football Club Annual 2001

31

The Wee General commanding his troops from the dugout

On 1 June 1998, Dick Advocaat joined **Rangers** as head coach, succeeding Walter Smith. He began his coaching career with Dutch amateur side DSVP in 1982. Two years later he became assistant coach to Rinus Michels, the national team manager. In 1987 he was appointed manager of the Haarlem club, then in 1989 became coach at Dordrecht where the director of football was Wim Jansen. In their first season, the pair won promotion to the First Division. In 1992, Advocaat replaced Michels as national team coach and led the Dutch team to a quarter final place in the 1994 World Cup. After the World Cup, he became coach at PSV Eindhoven. In 1996, he won the Dutch championship, ending the dominance of Ajax – indeed Eindhoven won the Dutch double of league and cup that season.

Advocaat is without doubt one of the most highly rated coaches in world football. The "Wee General", as he is affectionately known, immediately set about revitalising a club which had just lost the league on the last day of the season and had also lost the Scottish Cup to Hearts. For one reason or another, Richard Gough, Brian Laudrup, Ally McCoist, Stuart McCall, Andy Goram, Ian Durrant and Alex Cleland left the club, leaving Dick Advocaat with a very small

squad. Immediately he bought Arthur Numan and Giovanni van Bronckhorst from Holland: Numan cost £5 million and was at the time Holland's first choice left-back. Giovanni van Bronckhorst was a young midfielder with Feyenoord but much was expected of him in the future. After the World Cup, Advocaat went full ahead to sign players to build up his squad. In came Colin Hendry from Blackburn for £4 million, Andrei Kanchelskis from Fiorentina for £4.5 million, Gabriel Amato, the Argentinian forward from Real Mallorca for £4.5 million, Lionel Charbonnier, the 3rd choice goalkeeper for the 1998 World Cup winners France, and much to everyone's surprise, Rod Wallace on a free transfer from Leeds United.

Advocaat's first match in charge almost turned into a disaster when **Rangers** kicked off their UEFA Cup campaign against Shelbourne and were at one point 3-0 down, eventually winning 5-3. **Rangers** lost the opening match of the new Scottish Premier League 2-1 at Hearts. However, the Wee General was quick to mould a team pattern and results soon followed. Central to his plans was Barry Ferguson who was plucked from the **Rangers** reserves and given the role of central midfielder. A demanding role perhaps,

but Advocaat had watched Barry on video tapes before joining **Rangers** and liked what he saw. **Rangers** were strengthened further by the mid-season purchases of Neil McCann, Stefan Klos and Claudio Reyna.

Domestically, **Rangers** were in great shape for the majority of the 1998-99 season although they did have the slip-up of a 5-1 defeat by Celtic at Parkhead and the form did dip in the run-in. However, a great **Rangers** win against Aberdeen at home in April set them up nicely for a title decider at Parkhead on 2 May and the team did not disappoint! **Rangers** went there knowing that victory would secure the title and ran out easy winners 3-0 thanks to goals from Neil McCann (2) and Jorg Albertz going on to complete the domestic Treble (they had already won the Scottish League Cup by defeating St Johnstone 3-1) by beating Celtic 1-0 in the Scottish Cup Final thanks to a Rod Wallace goal. **Rangers**' European form also improved, gone were the batterings and humiliations and in came a new found resilience and organisation. After Shelbourne, **Rangers** put out PAOK Salonika (victors over Arsenal the previous season), Beyter Jerusalem, Bayer Leverkusen before finally losing out to Parma in the 3rd round of the UEFA Cup. So Dick Advocaat's first season ended in success: a domestic Treble, respectable results in Europe and a chance to enter the 1999-2000 Champion's League – he also signed a 2 year extension of his contract in the week leading up to the Scottish Cup Final.

The 1999-2000 season kicked off with **Rangers** signing Michael Mols from FC Utrecht and Dariusz Adamczuk from Dundee but all other transfers were put on hold unless players could be moved out. **Rangers** were handed early Champion's League action by drawing FC Haka of Finland. **Rangers** easily beat Haka over the 2 legs with Michael Mols scoring an excellent goal in the first leg, giving everyone a glimpse of what he could offer. **Rangers** were to beat Parma 2-0 at Ibrox in the next round, easing themselves into the group stages of the Champion's League. **Rangers** were drawn against PSV Eindhoven, Bayern Munich and Valencia and narrowly missed out on a place in the next stage after beating PSV home and away, losing to Valencia home and away and drawing and losing to Bayern Munich. The most impressive game was the 4-1 defeat of PSV at Ibrox but for many the defeat in Munich caught the eye with an outstanding performance against a Munich team who were very fortunate to go through. The night was marred by the loss of Michael Mols with cruciate ligament damage which ruled him out of the season. The great Euro dream ended in December in Dortmund in the UEFA Cup with **Rangers** losing out to Borussia Dortmund on penalties.

Domestically, **Rangers** topped the League at the start of the season and stayed there throughout the year. Celtic occasionally challenged but thanks to the brilliance of Dick Advocaat and his players, Celtic never got within touching distance of **Rangers**. The first Old Firm game of the season ended in a 4-2 win to **Rangers**; the New Year game ended in a 1-1 draw, the vital game in early February was won 1-0 thanks to a late Rod Wallace goal and the final game was a more than convincing 4-0 win at Ibrox. The 1999-2000 Championship was won after Celtic could only draw 1-1 with Hibs on 22 April with icing on the cake in a 2-0 win against St Johnstone the following day. **Rangers** played the Scottish Cup Final on May 27 2000, crushing Aberdeen 4-0.

So there we have it, the story of the Wee General at Ibrox to date. Five trophies out of six, but more importantly respect in Europe. After just two years in the job, Dick Advocaat has won over the Ibrox fans whose, wearing of Dutch national shirts at the Scottish Cup Final in tribute shows that they regard him as "SIMPLY THE BEST"! ❏

SCOTTISH PREMIER

claim the treble of League, Scottish FA Cup and League Cup!

LEAGUE CHAMPIONS!

1999/2000 SEASON REVIEW
PART TWO

CONTINUED FROM PAGE 11

JANUARY 2000 — **Rangers** returned from their winter break in Florida fully refreshed and free from any major injuries, and set about dismantling Aberdeen in great style at Ibrox. The visitors played it tight in the first 30 minutes but once **Rangers** found a breakthrough, they rattled in three goals before half time. The first goal was a bullet header from Craig Moore, very reminiscent of Terry Butcher or Mark Hateley. He spiced up his celebrations by running along the touch line and gesturing to the rows of Aberdeen fans to keep quiet! Apparently, according to certain newspapers, this could have caused a riot! Goals two and three followed very quickly with Arthur Numan getting his first ever goal for the Ibrox club. The second half was pretty much a stroll, with Rod Wallace and Barry Ferguson both getting on the score sheet.

Next up was a trip to Perth for the Sky-televised Scottish Cup tie. The conditions were pretty horrible with torrential rain but **Rangers** put in an assured performance and never looked like losing. Goals from Arthur Numan (a right-foot shot) and Giovanni van Bronckhorst sealed the tie.

Off the field, Seb Rozental was granted his work permit to allow him to return to Scotland after suffering three years of injury nightmare. He had spent the last year playing for his former club in Chile and appeared to have regained full fitness. With Rod Wallace still trying to regain his form of last season, Amato having being transferred to Gremio, and Jonatan Johansson and Michael Mols still injured, the need for a top class striker was very obvious. Marco Negri also returned to the **Rangers** team, playing in a 0-0 draw against Sparta Rotterdam but by all accounts he was still a long way short of the required fitness.

FEBRUARY 2000 — This was a strange month for **Rangers**. February started off well with an excellent victory at Tannadice but then was followed up with two away draws at Easter Road and then McDiarmid Park. Against Hibs, **Rangers** twice came

Sebastian Rozental fires a volley goalwards in the cup game against Ayr

from behind to earn the points while at McDiarmid Park, a wondergoal from Tony Vidmar looked set to net Rangers all three points until St Johnstone claimed a share of the spoils with a late equaliser. The Scottish Cup tie at Morton was only significant because it marked the return of Marco Negri who played the entire second half in an otherwise dreary and uninspiring game.

Just as it looked as if **Rangers** would be hitting a potentially harmful bad patch in the League, particularly with two games against Celtic coming

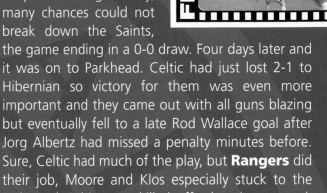

FLIXPIX

up, confidence was restored after a devastating 7-1 victory at Dens Park. What was significant was that **Rangers** ran into a 6-1 lead by half time, although understandably they could not maintain that momentum in the second half. The Dundee game also marked the full return of Sebastian Rozental from his injury hell and he topped off a fine performance with a goal.

So February ended with **Rangers** four League points clear and through to the 4th Round of the Scottish Cup. February was also the month when

Celtic lost 3-1 at home to First Division Inverness Caledonian Thistle, a club who had only recently been elected to the Scottish Football League. March promised to be an important month and Rangers did not disappoint ...

MARCH 2000 — March was a very significant month. Celtic's title hopes were faltering badly and only victory in both Old Firm matches would keep alive their hopes. **Rangers** started off the month with a dose of the jitters against St Johnstone and

despite having many, many chances could not break down the Saints, the game ending in a 0-0 draw. Four days later and it was on to Parkhead. Celtic had just lost 2-1 to Hibernian so victory for them was even more important and they came out with all guns blazing but eventually fell to a late Rod Wallace goal after Jorg Albertz had missed a penalty minutes before. Sure, Celtic had much of the play, but **Rangers** did their job, Moore and Klos especially stuck to the task, and Celtic were killed off when it mattered. Perfect tactics! On 8 March 2000, Stefan Klos emerged as a goalkeeper of real class and stature and his saves from Viduka went a long way to ensuring that the points went to Ibrox.

Next up was a Scottish Cup tie against Hearts in which **Rangers** strolled into an early lead, let Hearts back into the game and then finished them off in the second half. The game was not without controversy when it looked as if Lorenzo Amoruso might have been sent off for fouling Darren Jackson. Back to League business against Motherwell, and **Rangers** ran out easy winners but it wasn't an easy path to victory. Motherwell took an early lead but Rod Wallace emerged as **Rangers**' saviour with a hat trick of headers to seal victory.

The final match of the month saw Celtic visit Ibrox and while we heard the usual noises about how it would be different this time for Viduka etc, the outcome was somewhat different and spectacular. Albertz headed **Rangers** into the lead within a minute and even though **Rangers** had all of the first half play, it wasn't until just before half time that Andrei Kanchelskis made it 2-0.

The second half was a delight to watch, with **Rangers** playing some excellent football and the only "disappointment" was the failure to convert all the chances into goals. Eventually **Rangers**' superiority was turned into goals with late strikes from Albertz and the splendid Giovanni van Bronckhorst. No doubt about it, this was an absolute thumping and Celtic were very fortunate to get off with a 4-0 defeat. So March ended with the Premier League all but tied up.

APRIL 2000 — April was a busy month which saw **Rangers** top the League and reach the Scottish Cup final. First up was a visit to Aberdeen, never an easy place to go because The Dons always seem to raise their game against **Rangers** and this time was no different. Still, a draw did no harm to the League championship race and **Rangers** went home with their lead at the top still very healthy.

Next up were Dundee United at Ibrox and despite being 0-0 at half time, **Rangers** soon tied the game up in the 2nd half after the customary rousing Advocaat team-talk at half time. Next was the Scottish Cup semi final and despite the rather large score line (7-1 to **Rangers**!), this was not a stroll early on and only bad luck prevented Ayr United taking an early lead. Ayr regretted missing those chances and once **Rangers** gained control of the game there was no going back. Back to the Scottish Premier League and **Rangers** were drawing ever closer to Two in a Row, thanks to two fine away victories over Hearts and Dundee United. Ironically, victory for **Rangers** was clinched by Celtic failing to win against Hibs on 22 April and so the visit to St Johnstone the following day turned out to be a formality rather than the League clincher. The League trophy was presented to **Rangers** the following Sunday when Dundee, the only team to beat **Rangers** domestically all season, were the visitors. A fine victory rounded off a great evening's celebrations and Lorenzo Amoruso was presented with the Scottish Premier League trophy for the second year running. Overall, April was an excellent month with **Rangers** relentless in their successful pursuit of victory.

— May began much as April had ended with Dick Advocaat making it perfectly clear in his programme notes in the game against Hibernian that complacency would simply not be tolerated. He wrote: "Everyone in the squad is fighting for their Cup final place so I would expect nothing less than 100 per cent from my players from now until the end of the season."

The players seemed to respond with a convincing home win against Hibs. First half strikes from Ferguson and Dodds seemed to have secured maximum points for **Rangers** and a Dennis own goal just two minutes after the restart put the result beyond doubt. Hibernian though, fought back bravely through Miller and Lehman and had **Rangers** on the rack for a while. A Jorg Albertz brace however, in the last ten minutes settled any jangling nerves and normal service was resumed.

Next up was a Sunday trip to Rugby Park, Kilmarnock. Many of the usual starting line-up were either rested or injured and **Rangers'** fielded a weakened side. Both teams huffed and puffed their way towards the break occasionally sparking into life though generally flattering to deceive. But with just two minutes of the half remaining Claudio Reyna broke the deadlock capping a well constructed move with a wonderful piece of control and tidy finish.

The second 45 minutes was a brighter affair with both teams going close, Jonatan Johansson missing a couple of great chances after coming on as a substitute. Once again though it was to be Albertz who would seal the points for the 'Gers, crashing home a thirty yard thunderbolt in accustomed manner. **Rangers** enviable away form looking like it would last the season.

The penultimate game of the Scottish Premier League campaign was to be against third placed Hearts and as usual they were in stubborn mood and proved to be no pushover. This combined with **Rangers'** increasingly sluggish approach led to a rather drab game, hard fought though it was. Indeed, a well taken effort from Billy Dodds on twenty two minutes was to be all that separated the two sides at the end of ninety minutes. Another somewhat average performance from **Rangers'** was again good enough to claim full points, stretching their lead in the League to an impressive 24 points.

The last League game of the season at Motherwell was, amazingly, **Rangers'** first defeat away from home in the entire League season, the law of averages at last being proved true. Two second half strikes from Twaddle and Spencer (64 and 71 minutes respectively) were enough to take all the points. The poor performance had Advocaat leaping energetically from the dugout on numerous occasions. The title though had long since been captured and **Rangers'** can be forgiven for the tail off in their form. It was a shame however that **Rangers'** failed to pass the 100 league goals barrier eventually coming up just four short, an aim for this season perhaps!

The Scottish FA Cup Final on 27 May 2000 was to be the last game of the season and gave **Rangers'** the chance to complete an FA Cup and Premier League double. Also, if **Rangers** could

win the game it would clinch the club's 100th trophy in their illustrious history – a quite remarkable achievement!

The encounter was brought to life with **Rangers'** first attack of the match, Rod Wallace accidently colliding with Aberdeen 'keeper Jim Leighton. The injury sustained by Leighton instantly appeared to be serious and was later diagnosed as a fractured jaw. Aberdeen had opted not to select a goalkeeper as a substitute and, after some lengthy discussions, gave the number one shirt to Robbie Winters, who is more familiar with scoring goals rather than preventing them. This unfortunate sequence of events made the game something of no contest and it came as no surprise when Giovanni van Bronckhorst opened **Rangers'** account from an Albertz free kick. Dick Advocaat though, was obviously not satisfied with his side's application and **Rangers** began the second half in much brisker fashion.

Unsurprisingly Winters' frailties from crosses became increasingly apparent, a half cleared corner was returned to Vidmar who neatly controlled before banging his left foot drive past the spirited substitute goalkeeper. **Rangers** third followed soon after from another Albertz corner this time being more directly dispatched by Billy Dodds with a back post header. Jorg 'The Hammer' Albertz was to complete the scoring with a screaming drive from forty yards. Winters managed to tip the ball on to the bar but unluckily for the Pittodrie team the ball's momentum carried it over the line completing a thoroughly miserable day for Aberdeen.

Rangers' supporters though, can have no such gripes with their side, who were quite simply head and shoulders above the rest of the League - even on their off days. Two domestic titles is a sure sign of dominance in any country. With some excellent close season signings strengthening the squad and more transfer action promised who knows what 2001 will bring. The European Champion's League perhaps!!! ❏

SCOTTISH PREMIER LEAGUE 1999/2000 FINAL STANDINGS

Teams	P	W	L	D	GF	GA	Pts	GD
Rangers	36	28	6	2	96	26	90	+70
Celtic	36	21	6	9	90	38	69	+52
Hearts	36	15	9	12	47	40	54	+7
Motherwell	36	14	10	12	49	63	52	-14
St. Johnstone	36	10	1	14	36	44	42	-8
Hibernian	36	10	11	15	49	61	41	-12
Dundee	36	12	5	19	45	64	41	-19
Dundee Utd.	36	11	6	19	34	57	39	-23
Kilmarnock	36	8	13	15	38	52	37	-14
Aberdeen	36	9	6	21	44	83	33	-39

European Cup	FC Haka	1-4	Rangers	28-07-1999
Scottish Premier	Rangers	2-1	Kilmarnock	31-07-1999
European Cup	Rangers	3-0	FC Haka	04-08-1999
Scottish Premier	Hearts	0-4	Rangers	07-08-1999
European Cup	Rangers	2-0	Parma	11-08-1999
Scottish Premier	Rangers	4-1	Motherwell	15-08-1999
Scottish Premier	Rangers	4-1	Dundee Utd.	21-08-1999
European Cup	Parma	1-0	Rangers	25-08-1999
Scottish Premier	Hibernian	0-1	Rangers	28-08-1999
Scottish Premier	Rangers	3-0	Aberdeen	11-09-1999
European Cup	Valencia	2-0	Rangers	15-09-1999
European Cup	Rangers	1-1	B. Munich	21-09-1999
Scottish Premier	Rangers	3-1	St. Johnstone	25-09-1999
European Cup	PSV Eindhoven	0-1	Rangers	28-09-1999
Scottish Premier	Dundee	2-3	Rangers	02-10-1999
Scottish League Cup	Rangers	1-0	Dunfermline	12-10-1999
Scottish Premier	Kilmarnock	1-1	Rangers	16-10-1999
European Cup	Rangers	4-1	PSV Eindhoven	20-10-1999
European Cup	Rangers	1-2	Valencia	26-10-1999
Scottish Premier	Aberdeen	1-5	Rangers	30-10-1999
European Cup	B. Munich	1-0	Rangers	03-11-1999
Scottish Premier	Rangers	4-2	Celtic	07-11-1999
Scottish Premier	Rangers	2-0	Hibernian	20-11-1999
UEFA Cup	Rangers	2-0	B. Dortmund	25-11-1999
Scottish Premier	Rangers	1-2	Dundee	28-11-1999
Scottish League Cup	Aberdeen	1-0	Rangers	01-12-1999
UEFA Cup	B. Dortmund	2-0	Rangers	07-12-1999
Scottish Premier	Rangers	1-0	Kilmarnock	11-12-1999
Scottish Premier	Motherwell	1-5	Rangers	18-12-1999
Scottish Premier	Rangers	1-0	Hearts	22-12-1999
Scottish Premier	Celtic	1-1	Rangers	27-12-1999
Scottish Premier	Rangers	5-0	Hearts	22-01-2000
Scottish FA Cup	St. Johnstone	0-2	Rangers	30-01-2000
Scottish Premier	Dundee Utd.	0-4	Rangers	02-02-2000
Scottish Premier	Hibernian	2-2	Rangers	06-02-2000
Scottish Premier	St. Johnstone	1-1	Rangers	15-02-2000
Scottish FA Cup	Morton	0-1	Rangers	19-02-2000
Scottish Premier	Dundee	1-7	Rangers	27-02-2000
Scottish Premier	Rangers	0-0	St. Johnstone	04-03-2000
Scottish Premier	Celtic	0-1	Rangers	08-03-2000
Scottish FA Cup	Rangers	4-1	Hearts	12-03-2000
Scottish Premier	Rangers	6-2	Motherwell	18-03-2000
Scottish Premier	Rangers	4-0	Celtic	26-03-2000
Scottish Premier	Aberdeen	1-1	Rangers	01-04-2000
Scottish Premier	Rangers	3-0	Dundee Utd.	04-04-2000
Scottish FA Cup	Ayr	0-7	Rangers	08-04-2000
Scottish Premier	Hearts	1-2	Rangers	12-04-2000
Scottish Premier	Dundee Utd.	0-2	Rangers	15-04-2000
Scottish Premier	St. Johnstone	0-2	Rangers	23-04-2000
Scottish Premier	Rangers	3-0	Dundee	30-04-2000
Scottish Premier	Rangers	5-2	Hibernian	03-05-2000
Scottish Premier	Kilmarnock	0-2	Rangers	07-05-2000
Scottish Premier	Rangers	1-0	Hearts	13-05-2000
Scottish Premier	Motherwell	2-0	Rangers	21-05-2000
Scottish FA Cup	Aberdeen	0-4	Rangers	27-05-2000

1999/2000 RESULTS

HEADLINERS

The tabloid reporters have been very busy following the Rangers players around but have been unable to find anything to fill their pages. In a desperate attempt to please their bad-tempered editors they have concocted some stories and have mixed up the names of some of the Rangers players in the headlines. See if you can spot which player has been used in the headlines below:

ALL AND SUNDRY JOIN HONEST JONES'! ❶

SCOTTISH WILDMAN'S SONG HITS NUMBER ONE ❷

MARVELLOUS COW NEARS GRIMSBY! ❸

ROUND WALLS GIVE ACE VIEWS! ❹

ART HUNGRY NUN MANAGES GALLERY! ❺

STEAM FAN TAKES LOST TRACK! ❻

CHECK PAGE 64 FOR THE ANSWERS TO SEE IF YOU ARE RIGHT!

DARIUSZ ADAMCZUK

DARIUSZ ADAMCZUK

Height: 1.80m — **Weight:** 82kg
Date of Birth: 21/10/69
Place of Birth: Szczecin (Poland)
Signed From: Dundee in June 1999
Previous Clubs: Legia Warsaw, Eintracht Frankfurt, Udinese, Belenenses, Dundee
Position: Defender
Squad Number: 28
International Caps: 11 – Poland

There was a lot of speculation about Dariusz Adamczuk's move from Dundee as he had offers from both of the Old Firm sides.

Eventually he was snapped up by **Rangers**, under the Bosman ruling, in the summer of 1999. The self-assured Adamczuk has proved to be a real challenge to Sergio Porrini in the right-back position, but fitness problems meant that Dariusz lost his position for the Parma game.

However, his performances in pre-season matches showed that Adamczuk is comfortable in possession and an able tackler. His skill and flexibility mark the Polish international out as a very versatile and promising member of the **Rangers** squad. ❑

Kenny Miller signed for **Rangers** from Hibernian on a 5-year deal in a £2 million dream move.

Dick Advocaat has always said he would try to sign as many quality Scottish players as he could and proved his point by capturing Miller, widely considered one of the hottest young players in Scotland at the present time.

'He is a very promising player,' admitted Advocaat, 'And is very talented, although he still has to prove himself at a higher level.' Advocaat is sure to bring out the

KENNY MILLER

best in the 20-year-old striker, who is currently on the verge of international selection and was named Young Scottish Player of the Year last season.

Miller broke into the First Team at Hibernian in the last campaign following a loan spell at Stenhousemuir and scored two goals against **Rangers** at Easter Road when the Ibrox team drew 2-2 against the Edinburgh outfit last season.

His early appearances for **Rangers** have already confirmed him as a special talent. ❏

KENNY MILLER

Height: 1.78m
Weight: 71.7kg
Date of Birth: 23/12/79
Place of Birth: Edinburgh (Scotland)
Signed From: Hibernian in July 2000 for £2 million
Previous Clubs: Hibernian
Position: Forward — Squad Number: 23
International Caps: None

ALLAN JOHNSTON

ALLAN JOHNSTON

Height: 1.79m — Weight: 73.4kg
Date of Birth: 14/12/73
Place of Birth: Glasgow (Scotland)
Signed From: Sunderland July 2000, free transfer under Bosman ruling
Previous Clubs: Sunderland, Hearts, Rennes
Position: Forward
Squad Number: 24
International Caps: 9 – Scotland

Former Hearts player Johnston finally became a **Rangers** player on 1 July 2000 when he moved from Sunderland under the Bosman ruling.

Johnston had been frozen out at Sunderland since early in the season after changing his mind about signing a new contract, amid rumours of an approach from **Rangers**.

Johnston had a loan spell with Birmingham this season and he enjoyed a similar spell at Bolton.

He is expected to challenge Andrei Kanchelskis for the right-wing spot this season although he can also play on the left-wing or through the middle.

After signing **Rangers'** pre-contract agreement, Johnston said: 'Everyone knows I have supported **Rangers** since I was a boy. This is a dream come true for me.' ❑

Lionel Charbonnier

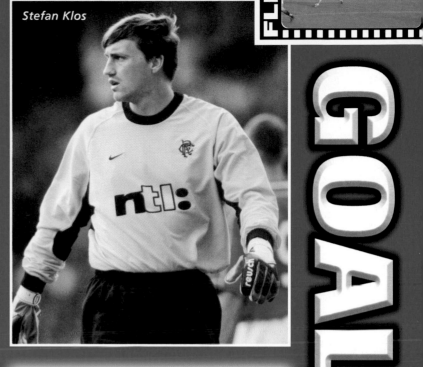

Stefan Klos

Stefan Klos signed for **Rangers** on Christmas Eve 1998 after a month-long contract dispute with Dortmund was finally resolved.

Klos went straight into the team, making his debut in the 1-0 win over St Johnstone in the Premier League on Boxing Day 1998. He kept his place for the rest of the season and amassed eleven clean sheets in just 23 games as he collected three winner's medals in his first season at Ibrox.

Before arriving in Glasgow, Klos helped Dortmund win the German Bundesliga twice, and amassed a great deal of experience in European competition. A knee injury and then a broken arm kept Klos out for a number of weeks but he returned to the First Team in time to kick off the second half of last season. ❑

STEFAN KLOS

Height: 1.83m
Weight: 88kg
Date of Birth: 16/07/71
Place of Birth: Germany
Signed From: Borussia Dortmund in 1998 for £700,000
Previous Clubs: Borussia Dortmund
Position: Goalkeeper — Squad Number: 1
International Caps: None

Charbonnier was signed from Auxerre, after 11 seasons there, for £1.2 million in the summer of 1998. He had his first taste of Ibrox when Auxerre beat **Rangers** 2-1 in the 1996-97 Champion's League and decided then he wanted to move to Glasgow, swayed by the 'whole atmosphere of Ibrox'. Charbonnier made his **Rangers** debut in the 2-1 League victory over Motherwell in August 1998. But after making 19 consecutive appearances in goal, Charbonnier was struck by the injury curse that hit the **Rangers'** goalkeepers last season. Damage to the ligaments in his left knee required surgery and ruled him out for the rest of the campaign. ❑

LIONEL CHARBONNIER

Height: 1.83m
Weight: 80kg
Date of Birth: 25/10/66
Place of Birth: Poitiers (France)
Signed From: AJ Auxerre (France) in July 1998 for £1.2 million
Previous Clubs: AJ Auxerre
Position: Goalkeeper — Squad Number: 30
International Caps: 1 – France

GOALKEEPERS

FLIXPIX

SEBASTIAN ROZENTAL

Height: 1.79m — **Weight:** 81kg
Date of Birth: 01/09/76
Place of Birth: Santiago (Chile)
Signed From: Universidad Catolica in 1997
for £3.8 million
Previous Club: Universidad Catolica
Position: Forward
Squad Number: 22

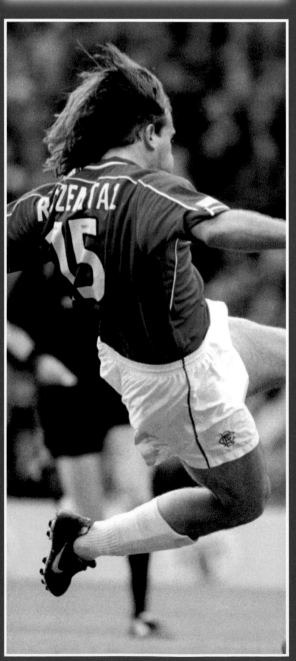

Sebastian Rozental is another player who scored on his **Rangers** debut, in the 3rd Round of the Scottish Cup against St Johnstone in January 1997. He was signed to **Rangers** for £3.8 million from Universidad Catolica in Chile. However, much of his time since his move to **Rangers** has been plagued with injury problems and the Ibrox faithful have yet to see the best from this quality striker. In fact, Rozental's injury nightmares began in his debut game as a knee problem meant that he was substituted at half time. There followed major treatment on what was diagnosed as medial ligament damage in his left knee. After three operations and three short appearances as a substitute in the Premiership, he had a fourth operation and returned to his old team in Chile on an 18-month extended loan.

Rozental re-joined his **Rangers** teammates at their Florida training camp in the mid-season break last year and Dick Advocaat recalled him from his loan. Fully fit, he began to show what he could do in the second half of the season, scoring in the 7-1 defeat of Dundee in February and in the 6-2 victory over Motherwell in March. The fans were pleased to see him back.

Rozental remained in the **Rangers** First Team squad for the rest of last season and happily was injury free. This year he will be aiming for a regular First Team slot and we wish him the best. ❏

Claudio Reyna joined **Rangers** near the end of the 1998/99 season from German side Wolfsburg, where he had been captain. Dick Advocaat saw Reyna as the perfect player to strengthen his midfield and to add a little experience to help younger players like Barry Ferguson.

By the time Reyna came to Ibrox, he had already amassed a total of 65 international caps for the USA and had represented his country at the Olympics in Barcelona in 1992 and in two World Cup campaigns. He also had the honour of captaining his national team and was awarded the 'USA Player of the Decade'.

The American's Ibrox career began superbly as he scored three goals in the first two Premier League games against Kilmarnock and Hearts. He also scored the vital second goal in the First Leg of the Champion's League qualifier with Parma. Reyna is a versatile player who has a fantastic engine and who allies his work rate with great skill. Last season he made 38 appearances for **Rangers**, mostly in midfield, but he is equally capable of filling in at right-back when needed

Reyna is pictured above right with his son, celebrating the Scottish Cup victory over Aberdeen, and there is every chance that this young man will be a fine footballer in his own right, especially as Claudio's wife, Danielle, is a USA international soccer star in her own right, with a total of 20 caps!   ❏

CLAUDIO REYNA

Height: 1.77m — Weight: 73.2kg
Date of Birth: 20/07/73
Place of Birth: New Jersey (USA)
Signed From: Wolfsburg (Germany)
in 1999 for £2 million
Previous Clubs: Bayer Leverkusen,
Wolfsburg
Position: Midfield — Squad Number: 12
International Caps: 72 – USA

Rangers

ACROSS

1 and 27. Who scored all the goals in a 4-1 thrashing of Motherwell in August 1999? (7, 4)

3 . _ _ _ _ _ _ Charbonnier, France's 3rd choice goalkeeper who is great at making **24 DOWN**s? (6)

8. How many points did **RANGERS** amass in the 1998/1999 Scottish League? (7, 5)

10. A top striker who isn't the joker in the pack but is a goal _ _ _. (3)

11. He signed from Dundee United for £1.3 million. (5)

12. The **RANGERS** v Celtic match is known all around the world as the OLD _ _ _ _ derby. (4)

15. Who did **RANGERS** beat in the 2nd round of the 1998/1999 UEFA Cup? PAOK _ _ _ _ _ _ _ _ (8)

16. You might see a big celebration if Michael Mols had just _ _ _ _ _ _. (6)

20. Everybody at Ibrox knows him as 'The Hammer'. (7)

21. What is Penttila's first name? (4)

22. Who did **RANGERS** beat in the 1972 Cup Winner's Cup Final? (6, 6)

26. The post you would run to if you were going to flick on a header? (4)

28. Allan Johnston arrived from Sunderland on a _ _ _ _ transfer under the Bosman ruling. (4)

29. Jonatan Johansson scored how many goals in the 5-1 win over Aberdeen last season? (5)

DOWN

1. You might hold your head in your hands if you had had a 'goal'den opportunity and did this – opposite of 16 across. (6)

2. We're playing at _ _ _ _ when we're playing at Ibrox Park. (4)

3. In **RANGERS**' game against Aberdeen on April Fool's day 2000 the scores finished what? (5)

4. Dutch Defender and pop star of the 70s and 80s. Ask your mum or dad if you're stuck! (5)

5. Which Dane, whose previous clubs are AB Copenhagen and Akademisk Boldklub chose to sign for **RANGERS** this summer ahead of many English Premiership sides? (11)

6. Who were the official sponsors of both **RANGERS** and Celtic last season? (3)

7. Paul Ritchie was obtained free on the Bosman ruling. But from which club did he sign? (6)

9. Who scored the opening goal against Dundee United in the 4-0 away win this February? (6)

12. Gordon Strachan, the Coventry City manager, offered how many millions for Neil McCann? (4)

13. From the same country as Harry Kewell, Mark Bosnich and **RANGERS**' Tony Vidmar, a defender who impressed last season? (5)

14 and 21. What was the score in the game against Kilmarnock in May 2000? (3, 3)

16. What is Billy Dodds' squad number this season? (7)

17. What is the position of Scott Wilson, Lorenzo Amoruso and Craig Moore? (8)

18. Who scored **RANGERS** first hat trick of the millennium (against Dundee in February)? (7)

19. Name the living legend and TV personality who is **RANGERS**' top all-time goalscorer? (7)

23. If you suffered a dead leg when playing football it might feel _ _ _ _? (4)

26. If you cheer when **RANGERS** score you probably cheer when Stefan Klos makes a what? (4)

25. Dick Advocaat is also known as 'The _ _ _ General? (3)

FLIXPIX

Xword

Test your football knowledge by answering the clues and filling in the grid below.

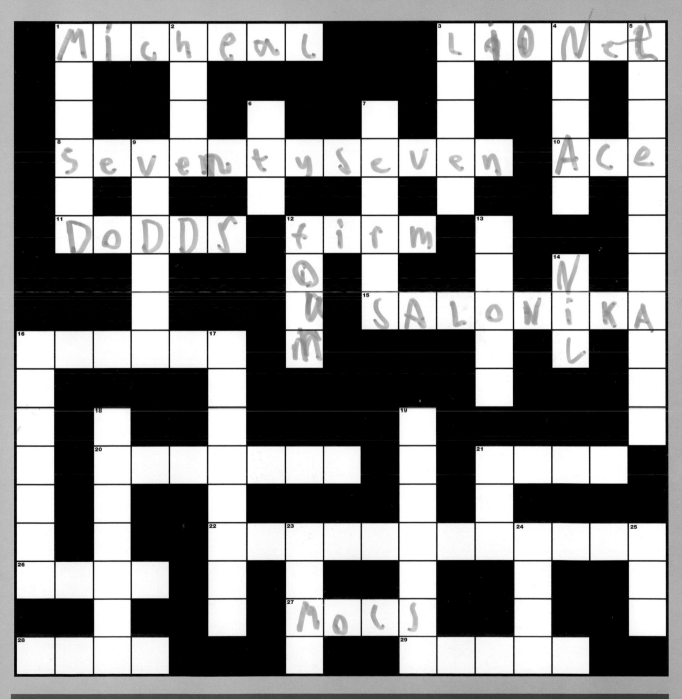

CHECK PAGE 64 FOR THE ANSWERS

RANGERS LEGENDS

GREATEST RANGER:
1. John Greig 2. Ally McCoist 3. Davie Cooper

GREATEST STRIKER:
Ally McCoist

GREATEST GOALKEEPER:
Andy Goram

GREATEST GOAL:
Davie Cooper against Celtic, Dryborough Cup Final 1979

GREATEST NON-SCOT:
Brian Laudrup

GREATEST TEAM:
Andy Goram, Sandy Jardine, John Greig, Richard Gough, Terry Butcher, Jim Baxter, Brian Laudrup, Paul Gascoigne, Ally McCoist, Mark Hateley and Davie Cooper

GREATEST CONTRIBUTION:
David Murray, Campbell Ogilvie and Willie Waddell

GEORGE YOUNG • 1941 to 1957

Appearances - 428   Goals - 31
6 League / 4 Scottish Cup / 2 League Cup Medals

Born in Grangemouth in 1922, George Young (nicknamed Corky because he carried around a champagne cork in his pocket for luck) was a commanding defender. He joined Rangers aged 15 and his first game was in November 1941 in a 3-2 victory over Falkirk. Over the years, he became a reliable penalty taker, scoring from the spot in the 2-2 draw with Moscow Dynamo in 1945. Although he started out as a centre-half, he switched to right-back after the war to allow Willie Woodburn to resume his regular position in the centre of defence.

Young had few weaknesses. He was commanding in the air, a strong tackler and for such a tall man (he was 6ft 2ins) remarkably quick on his feet. It annoyed Young that the Rangers team of that time were accused of playing 'route one' football, with Willie Thornton regularly scoring from his upfield clearances. In fact, this was an attacking ploy practised in training.

In 1957, after winning his 53rd cap for Scotland, Corky quit football. For a brief time in the 1960s, he managed Third Lanark. A few years later, the then Rangers Chairman John Paton refused to allow Young's testimonial match to be played at Ibrox and banned Rangers players from playing in it. The rift that resulted with the club

was not healed until 1992, when David Murray invited him to attend a Rangers match. He died a few years later and a minute's silence was observed in his memory during a Rangers versus Aberdeen match at Ibrox. Young will be remembered as one of the finest defenders of his era and a great Rangers Captain.

ALLY McCOIST • 1983 to 1998

Appearances - 583   Goals - 355
9 League / 1 Scottish Cup / 9 League Cup Medals

The former St. Johnstone and Sunderland striker was signed for Rangers by John Greig in 1983. His reign as Ibrox "Goal King" saw him go through four managers and over 40 striking partners. His Rangers career had a shaky start as the fans were not immediately impressed.

However, showing remarkable strength of character, Ally turned things around to become a legend. He is Rangers' all-time top scorer, has won two European Golden Boots and numerous medals, and he was awarded an MBE for services to Association Football - all this despite spending much of Graeme Souness' managerial tenure on the bench, earning himself the nickname "The Judge". Perhaps his greatest season was in 1992-93, with Rangers winning the Treble, narrowly missing out on a European Cup final and going 44 games unbeaten. He had scored 49 goals when he broke his leg during Scotland's match against Portugal.

His poacher's instinct has enabled him to score so many vital goals for the club, including Old Firm hat tricks, cup final winners and European goals, that a recent world-wide poll of Rangers fans voted Ally "Best Ever Rangers Striker" and second to John Greig as "Best Ever Ranger". He is now playing for Kilmarnock and is carving out a

niche as a TV personality. Rangers fans will remember him simply as "Super Ally".

JOHN GREIG • 1960 to 1978

Appearances - 755   Goals - 120
5 League / 6 Scottish Cups / 4 League Cup Medals

Although Greig finished his career as a left-back, he will be best remembered as a right half-back. He stayed with Rangers through good times and bad and was the only 'Gers captain to lift a European trophy when the team won the Cup Winners' Cup in Barcelona in 1972.

He was the glue that held the team together during the dark days of Celtic's dominance during the late 1960's and early 70's. He could have chosen to leave Rangers, indeed Spurs manager Bill Nicholson wanted to sign him, but he decided to stay and was inspirational in the rebirth of Rangers under Jock Wallace, winning trebles in 1976 and 1978.

When Jock Wallace shocked everyone by resigning in 1978, Greig was offered the job. He did not feel ready for it and had intended playing on for another few years, but he couldn't turn down the chance to manage Rangers.

In his very first season, the team won 2 cups and reached the last eight in Europe. But it became apparent that the team was ageing and major construction was needed. At this time, the New Firm of Aberdeen and Dundee United were emerging and the fans were unhappy by the club's lack of success. In 1983 he was replaced by Jock Wallace. He left football completely for seven years but was brought back to Ibrox by David Murray and Graeme Souness as PR Chief. He now helps out Dick Advocaat with the football side of the club. After spending 40 years at Rangers in various capacities (footballer, manager, PR Chief), Greig was recently voted "Best Ever Ranger" in a recent supporters poll. ❑

BERT KONTERMAN

Height: 1.89m — **Weight:** 85kg
Date of Birth: 14/01/71
Place of Birth: Rouveen (Holland)
Signed From: Feyenoord Rotterdam in July 2000 for £4.5 million
Previous Clubs: Feyenoord Rotterdam, SC Rouveen, PEC Zwolle, Cambuur, Willem II
Position: Defender — **Squad Number:** 15
International Caps: 11

Bert Konterman became the fifth Dutch signing of Advocaat's reign at **Rangers** in July 2000. His nickname at Feyenoord was King Kon. So we had all better watch out for some pretty fearsome tackles. He proved invaluable at the heart of Holland's defence at Euro 2000 so he should soon become favourite with the **Rangers** fans. ❑

FLIXPIX

Sergio Porrini joined **Rangers** during the summer of 1997 after playing in the European Cup Final for Juventus. The £3 million defender had played at Ibrox when the Turin side beat **Rangers** in the Champion's League in 1995.

It was in the qualifying round for the Champion's League that he made his **Rangers** debut in the 6-0 thrashing of Gl Gotu at the start of the 1996-97 season.

Porrini, born in Milan, began his career with his local club AC in 1988. As a 20-year-old, he found it difficult to break into the senior side and moved to Atalanta. He stayed there for four seasons, playing in 100 League games and scoring three goals.

The "big time" beckoned when he signed for Juventus. Apart from his European success, he played 87 games for them in Serie A, scoring once.

He scored his first goal for **Rangers**, a header, in the 2-2 draw with Motherwell in September 1997. And he missed only one game in the 1998-99 season as he claimed the most consistent appearance record of any player, with three goals in a massive 54 games. During an effective season, Porrini's only blemish was the red card he received when he returned to his home country to face Parma in the UEFA Cup. He made a total of 22 appearances last year. Porrini is an avid collector of club shirts. He has more than 250 of them. His favourites? Ronaldo's Inter Milan jersey and a Manchester United one worn by Eric Cantona. ❏

SERGIO PORRINI

Height: 1.81m — **Weight:** 79.5kg
Date of Birth: 8/11/68
Place of Birth: Milan (Italy)
Signed From: Juventus in June 1997 for £3.5 million
Previous Clubs: AC Milan, Atalanta, Juventus
Position: Defender — **Squad Number:** 21
International Caps: 2 – Italy

SERGIO PORRINI

PETER LOVENKRANDS

Height: 1.77m — **Weight:** 70kg
Date of Birth: 29/01/80
Place of Birth: Horsholm (Denmark)
Signed From: AB Copenhagen in July 2000 for £1.3 million
Previous Clubs: Akademisk Boldklub
Position: Forward
Squad Number: 26
International Caps: None

The players leave the field after being presented with the Premier League trophy

Forward Peter Lovenkrands was signed by **Rangers** for £1.5 million, having been chased by numerous Premiership clubs. Well done, Advocaat and Murray, as 20-year old Lovenkrands has been tipped for the very top.

Brian Laudrup has noticed Peter's something extra: 'Everyone in Denmark thinks he has the potential to be a star. He has always looked a special player when I have seen him in action.' Peter makes the admiration mutual as he professes: 'I sincerely hope that I can have part of the success that Brian Laudrup enjoyed at the club.'

Though different types of players, comparisons between Lovenkrands and Laudrup are inevitable as both came to **Rangers** from Denmark.

Peter's brother Tommy, six years his senior, has also come over to Scotland from Denmark. The brothers were a Danish equivalent of the Nevilles as both played for AB Copenhagen. Brotherly rivalry will come into play as the two of them look set to face each other when **Rangers** play St Johnstone this year. ❑

Arthur Numan probably knows **Rangers** manager Dick Advocaat better than most. He has played for him at three different clubs.

Numan was a young left-winger at Haarlem in 1988 when he was persuaded by Advocaat that he should move to left-back. This foresight paid off as Numan became a Dutch international and one of the best full-backs in Europe. Numan arrived at **Rangers** just two weeks after playing for Holland in the 1998 World Cup.

Numan was signed for £4.5 million from PSV Eindhoven where he had also played under Advocaat. He had been at PSV for six years and was part of Advocaat's team that won the Dutch League and Cup double in 1996. Numan also played for FC Twente before joining PSV.

He made his **Rangers** debut in the 2-0 UEFA Cup victory over Shelbourne and rounded off a

ARTHUR NUMAN

fine performance by winning the Man of the Match award. During the first half of the season, Numan proved himself to be a fine player, but he was forced out of action after chipping an ankle bone in the 1-0 win over Kilmarnock just before Christmas. The ankle did not respond to treatment and in February, Numan had an operation and was ruled out for the rest of that season. Numan said: 'It's a very bad ankle injury, one of the worst a footballer can get. It will take three or four months to recover so all I can do is look forward to the start of next season.' He returned for the home draw with Bayern Munich, but lasted only four games before injury struck again, this time against Dundee in early October. But that only kept him out for two weeks as he returned in late October. Numan scored his first goal for the club in the 5-0 win over Aberdeen. ❑

ARTHUR NUMAN

Height: 1.81m — Weight: 78.8kg
Date of Birth: 14/12/69
Place of Birth: Heemskerk (Holland)
Signed From: PSV Eindhoven in July 1998 for £4.5 million
Previous Clubs: Haarlem, FC Twente, PSV Eindhoven
Position: Defender — Squad Number: 5
International Caps: 40 – Holland

ROD WALLACE

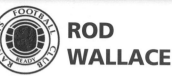

ROD WALLACE

Height: 1.72m — Weight: 70.8kg
Date of Birth: 02/10/69
Place of Birth: Lewisham (England)
Signed From: Leeds United in July 1998
as a free transfer
Previous Clubs: Southampton, Leeds United
Position: Striker
Squad Number: 10
International Caps: None

A revelation in his first season, Rod Wallace was another of **Rangers'** signings in the summer of 1998. It was a shrewd piece of business by manager Dick Advocaat.

Wallace was out of contract at Leeds and arrived at Ibrox for no transfer fee under the Bosman ruling. He was an instant success, scoring on his debut against Hearts on the opening day of the League season and going on to fire 27 goals in 51 appearances. As other, big money forwards struggled to settle at Ibrox, Wallace made the main striking role his own. He grabbed his first hat trick for the club on 28 February 1999 in a 5-0 win over Kilmarnock.

Born in Lewisham, South-East London, Rod joined Southampton as a 16-year-old trainee, making his League debut in the 1987-88 season. His two brothers, Danny and Ray, also had spells playing at the south coast club, moving on to Manchester United and Leeds United respectively. Rod scored 45 goals at the Dell in 128 League games, his best season being 1989-90 when he hit 18.

Craig Moore celebrates after scoring against Aberdeen

Tero Penttila was a surprise signing from FC Haka, a team **Rangers** comprehensively beat in the qualifying round for last year's Champion's League. The tall defender caught Dick Advocaat's eye during the two games and he made a £300,000 move in November 1999.

It is Penttila's first move into full-time football and he has had to put his studies at medical school on hold for the time being.

'Of course it is a bit of a surprise to be here. You can't say you played well when a team scores seven times against you. I am looking forward to playing in front of big crowds at Ibrox.'

Dick Advocaat was delighted to have secured the services of Penttila: 'Tero has a good touch, is good in the air and is very strong. He didn't cost much when you compare him to other players I have brought to the club. I think in style he is a bit like Thomas Helmer (the German international) and we will give him a chance, although it will take him time to settle in.' ❑

He was transferred to Leeds in 1991 for £1.6 million and won the English Championship in his first year with the club. Wallace, an England B international who scored 53 goals in 212 League games for Leeds, says brother Danny has always been the biggest influence on his career. On coming to **Rangers** he said: 'The size of the club is incredible, much bigger than Leeds and the supporters are second to none.'

Wallace began the new season as he ended his first, scoring **Rangers'** opening League goal against Kilmarnock at Ibrox. However, injury struck in the second leg of the Euro clash with Parma and a hamstring problem kept Wallace out until late September. After a difficult October, Advocaat rested him for the first Old Firm clash to help Wallace regain his sharpness. He was soon back to his best, though, and was a virtual ever present to the end of the campaign, grabbing a total of 20 goals including hat tricks against Motherwell and Dundee. ❑

TERO PENTTILA

Height: 1.88m
Weight: 81kg
Date of Birth: 09/03/75
Place of Birth: Finland
Signed From: FC Haka in October 1999
Previous Clubs: Re'pas, FC Kuusysi, FC Lahti, FC Haka
Position: Defender — Squad Number: 29
International Caps: None

TERO PENTTILA

FERNANDO RICKSEN

Height: 1.75m
Weight: 70.5kg
Date of Birth: 27/07/76
Place of Birth: Heerlen (Holland)
Signed From: AZ Alkmaar for £3.6 million
Previous Clubs: Fortuna Sittard, AZ Alkmaar
Position: Defender
Squad Number: 2
International Caps: None

Ricksen is another **Rangers** player who had his pick of English Premiership clubs. Ultimately, the 23-year-old chose to sign a five-year deal with **Rangers**.

Dick Advocaat has already coached Ricksen at youth level, before Fernando went on to captain the Dutch Under-23 side, and then to become one of the best defenders in Holland.

It seems that fellow Ibrox Dutchman Michael Mols might have been influential in Ricksen's decision to sign for **Rangers**. As Fernando himself says: 'When I first told Michael Mols that **Rangers** were interested in me, he told me not to even consider anything else, not to even look at the place but just go. He said it was perfect'.

Perfect or not, Mol's advice seems to have been sound as Ricksen has settled in happily, filling the problematical right-back role. Fernando says: 'I will do my best and work hard to fight for a place in the team.' Just the sort of determination we expect from a **Rangers** player! ❑

The Ibrox faithful show their appreciation for Dutch Manager Dick Advocaat

FLIXPIX

TONY VIDMAR

Vidmar signed from Dutch side NAC Breda where he made 62 League appearances in two seasons, scoring four goals.

Before that, he had played for Belgian side Germinal Ekeren and at home in Adelaide. Vidmar came to **Rangers** as a free agent under the Bosman ruling and made his debut in the 5-0 defeat of GI Gotu in a Champion's League qualifier in July 1997.

He played in 12 League games during his first season at Ibrox and has settled in as a regular contender for a place in **Rangers'** defence.

Vidmar scored his first goal for the Club with a header in the 6-0 rout of Hamilton in the Fourth Round of the Scottish Cup. He commented: 'It's always a great moment to score for your club and it's been a long time coming.'

A lengthy run in the team allowed Vidmar to show his true quality. His stunning, if unlikely, goal against Parma confirmed that Vidmar is a worthy member of the **Rangers** squad. ❏

TONY VIDMAR

Height: 1.87m — Weight: 79kg
Date of Birth: 04/07/70
Place of Birth: Adelaide (Australia)
Signed From: NAC Breda (Holland) in July 1997 as a free transfer
Previous Clubs: Adelaide City, Germinal Ekeren, NAC Breda
Position: Defender — Squad Number: 25
International Caps: 40 – Australia

SCOTT WILSON

Height: 1.90m
Weight: 83kg
Date of Birth: 19/03/77
Place of Birth: Edinburgh (Scotland)
Signed From: Product of Ibrox Youth Policy
Previous Clubs: None
Position: Defender
Squad Number: 19
International Caps: None

Scott Wilson made his **Rangers** debut in the 1996/97 UEFA Champion's League when he was only nineteen, lining up in central defence alongside Richard Gough as **Rangers** took on Ajax, Grasshoppers and Auxerre. He also made his first Premier League appearance that season, in the 4-3 victory over Hibs. Wilson, a product of the Ibrox youth system, has had to be patient, though, because of the fierce competition for First Team places.

However, he had been assured about his **Rangers** future by manager Dick Advocaat and he made his first start of the 1998-99 season in the thrilling 2-1 victory at Bayer Leverkusen in the UEFA Cup. He went on to make 20 appearances in that campaign, scoring his first goal and being sent off in the Old Firm derby.

By the end of that season he had earned a place in the Scottish Under-21 side and his development continued last year. Out of the team at the start of last season he fought his way into contention, appearing in nine consecutive games from 12 March to 23 April. ❏

CELEBRATION TIME
LEFT: *Andrei Kanchelskis and Barry Ferguson congratulate Billy Dodds;*
BELOW: *Lorenzo Amoruso cracks open a bottle of bubbly on another vintage season*

OFFICIAL
YOUNG SUPPORTERS
CLUB

Colour in ALBERTZ

Colour in this picture of Jorg Albertz using paints, crayons or coloured pencils.

ANSWERS

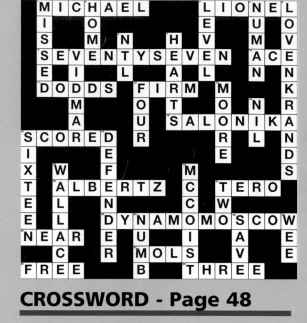

CROSSWORD - Page 48

SPOT THE BALL - Page 23

The ball is in square D1

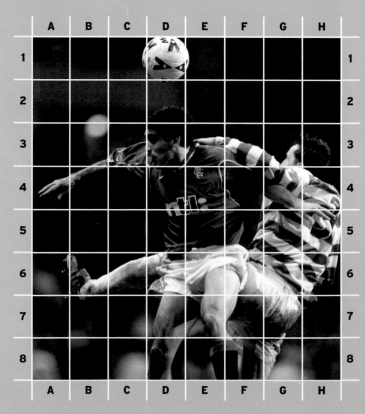

WORDSEARCH - Page 22

The missing Premier League side is DUNDEE UNITED, while the First Division team hiding in the grid is FALKIRK

HEADLINERS - Page 41

1   Alan Johnston
2   Scott Wilson
3   Marco Negri
4   Rod Wallace
5   Arthur Numan
6   Stefan Klos